In the time of your life, live – so that in that good time there shall be no ugliness or death for yourself or for any life your life touches. Seek goodness everywhere, and when it is found, bring it out of its hiding place and let it be free and un-ashamed.

The Time of Your Life

BREAKING BREAD

with

William Saroyan

by
Janice Stevens

watercolors by
Pat Hunter

BREAKING BREAD WITH WILLIAM SAROYAN ©2016 Janice Stevens and Pat Hunter

Production Assistance Provided by Heliograph Publishing
An Imprint of HBE Publishing

Layout and cover design by Christopher Estep / Dan Dunklee, Heliograph Publishing

Saroyan quotes used with permission Mimi Calter, Associate University Librarian & Chief of Staff

Stanford University Libraries

Armenian translation of Antranik of Armenia courtesy of Ani Grigoryan, MBA.

William Saroyan signature courtesy Personal Collection Dan Dunklee, Second Chances

Dinner at Omar Khayyam's with permission of Haig Mardikian

Library of Congress Control Number: in process
ISBN 978-1-943050-40-6 Hardcover

Printed in the United States of America
September 2016

HBE PUBLISHING

Dedication

In creating this book, we were struck by the compassion and tenacity of the Armenian people. The sense of family is dominant, be it blood or culture.

Sharing an important event, a meal, or just a cup of coffee was significant. It means accepting and belonging. For this reason, we humbly dedicate this work to the Armenian people, worldwide, whom William Saroyan personified.

J.S. and P.H.

"Give us this day our daily bread."
Matthew 6:11

Mr. MacGregor asked Tom Baker if he had a bit of sausage at his house and Tom said he did, and Mr. MacGregor asked Tom if it would be convenient for Tom to go and get that little bit of sausage and come back with it and when Tom returned Mr. MacGregor would play a song on the bugle that would change the whole history of Tom's life. And Tom went home for the sausage, and Mr. McGregor asked each of the eighteen good neighbors and friends if he had something small and nice to eat at his home and each man said he did, and each man went to his home to get the small and nice thing to eat, so Mr. MacGregor would play the song he said would be so wonderful to hear, and when all the good neighbors and friends had returned to our house with all the small and nice things to eat, Mr. MacGregor lifted the bugle to his lips and played My Heart's in the Highlands, My Heart is not Here, and each of the good neighbors and friends wept and returned to his home, and Mr. MacGregor took all the good things into the kitchen and our family feasted and drank and was merry: an egg, a sausage, a dozen green onions, two kinds of cheese, butter, two kinds of bread, boiled potatoes, fresh tomatoes, a melon, tea, and many other good things to eat, and we ate and our bellies tightened, and Mr. Mac-Gregor said, Sir, if it is all the same to you I should like to dwell in your house for some days to come, and my father said, Sir, my house is your house, and Mr. MacGregor stayed at our house seventeen days and nights….

The Man with the Heart in the Highlands, *Fresno Stories*

TABLE OF CONTENTS

FOREWORD

Dennis Elia

During William Saroyan's formative years, there were many upheavals. Born of immigrant parents, and with the early passing of his father, a courageous and proud mother was forced to send her three children to live for five years in an orphanage. When enough money was saved to regain custody, a sensitive youngster selling newspapers on the streets of Fresno emerged to eventually become one of the best storytellers of the times and toils of the everyday man.

Saroyan was a driven person, who avidly worked at his profession on his trusted manual Underwood typewriter until his last days.

He was well travelled, and wrote prolifically from many locales around the globe. Thus, he developed a fine palate for the local cuisine whether in San Francisco, Los Angeles, New York, Paris, London, Vienna, Odessa, Yerevan and elsewhere.

This book enables you to explore the same pleasures in dining that Saroyan experienced. From the starter dishes through the main courses, and on into the dessert selections, you can experience what Saroyan enjoyed. You will be able to peruse the authentic restaurant menu of New York's Golden Horn, and San Francisco's famous Omar Khayyam as experienced by William Saroyan.

Born of the Bitlis tribe in Western Armenia, Saroyan appreciated their penchant for all things related to the cabbage. Whether in the form of a hot or cold cabbage broth, sumptuous ground lamb cabbage rolls or boiled lambs-head soup, these authentic ethnic recipes are re-created for you to read and try.

In Paris, along with enjoying outstanding French cuisine, he sought out a tiny neighborhood restaurant, Le Diamantaire, that featured boiled sheep's-head soup. This particular main dish became his "signature dish" in regard to what he most enjoyed if it could be found in whatever city he was living or was visiting on the world stage.

An insight into Saroyan's character was that although many admirers both in his home town of Fresno and elsewhere, would quite often shower him with invitations to be a dinner guest, he was most reluctant to accept these invitations. Instead, he would prefer to make subtle inquiries as to who cooked the best specialty dish he desired and Saroyan would then proceed to call and ask to be invited to dinner. And in that fashion, it was the food, and not his celebrity that would be the focus of the evening.

The magic of Saroyan, was his ability to communicate "the message" in such a direct and simplistic manner. To be in his presence and engage him in conversation was so moving, that however jaded you were in conversing with the famous and powerful, you would never be able to forget how he would excite your auditory senses. I felt rewarded by the experience.

Hopefully, this well-researched and beautifully illustrated book will help you capture the essence of William Saroyan and the recipes that so delighted and satisfied his culinary indulgence.

If you are the adventurous type, take a chance and indulge, much as Saroyan.

I went to see. To find out. To breathe the air. To be in that place.

The grapes of the Armenian vineyards were not yet ripe, but there were fresh green leaves, and the vines were exactly like the vines of California, and the faces of the Armenians of Armenia were exactly like the faces of the Armenians of California. The rivers Arax and Kura moved slowly through the fertile earth of Armenia in the same way that the rivers King and San Joaquin moved though the valley of my birthplace. And the sun was warm and kindly, no less than the sun of California.

Yes gnats'i tesnel, parzel, shnch'yel ody, linel ayd vayrum:

Haystani aygineri khaghoghy der cher hasel, bayts' kayn t'arm kanach terevner, yev vazeri sharkery nman ein Kaliforniayi khaghoghi ayginerin, yev hayastants'ineri demk'ery nman ein Kaliforniayi hayeri demk'erin: Arax yev Kura getery dandagh hosum ein Hayastani ptghaber hogherov, inchpes King yev San Joaquin getery vor hosum ein im tsnndavayri dashterov: Yev arevy jerm er ou bari, voch' pakas Kaliforniayi arevits:

Antranik of Armenia, *Essential Saroyan*

Breaking Bread with William Saroyan

Janice Stevens

Born in August 1908, in Fresno California, William Saroyan referred to himself as an Armenian American and depicted the angst of an Armenian whose immigrant parents fled their homeland prior to the Genocide of 1915. William's father, Armenak, although a poet and preacher, worked in the vineyards of the Central Valley. After his father's untimely death, William, age three, and his siblings were placed in the Fred Finch Orphanage in Oakland, California while his mother, Takoohi, found employment in the packing houses.

The formative years spent in the orphanage took their toll on William. Too young to grasp the finality of his father's death and his mother's apparent abandonment, Saroyan's writings reflect the yearning he had in waiting for his father to return.

He writes,

> I began in earnest at the Fred Finch Orphanage in Oakland, California. I said goodbye to my mother and began.... The white pitcher full of cold milk and warm afternoons I remember. The cook's meat pies with the golden crust. The Sunday breakfast eggs, brown and white. The Marshall walks to

Sunday school. The witches in the hills. The hazelnuts in the trees. The ferns and the poison oak along the paths. The water dogs, captured and brought home. The blue bellied lizards which snapped off their tails in captivity. The climbing of the slim eucalyptus trees, making them bend to the earth again. The visiting tellers of tales. The German band on the steps of the Administration Building.

The Bicycle Rider in Beverly Hills

William wrote extensively of his Fresno roots. He portrayed a childhood growing up in a clustered community known as Armenian Town, after his mother, with the help of her brother, brought her children home. His literary work reveals a young boy growing to manhood, then as an adult experiencing success, and finally as an older man deeply rooted in the culture of his people.

Traditional gatherings of weddings, funerals, and holidays were shared with the community. These memories and images stayed with him throughout his life.

A celebration centered on food is an integral aspect of Armenian life. Using recipes handed down for generations, the Armenians Saroyan depicts in his literary expressions reflect the ethnicity common to his culture.

Ancient traditions are reenacted preserving centuries of culture. Traditional as well as religious holidays give cause for celebration featuring Armenian dishes. Fresno's Blessing of the Grapes, has been held annually for more than a hundred years. During one of those occasions, on

August 11, 2000, Western Prelate Archbishop Moushegh Mardirossian celebrated the Divine Liturgy, saying, "The importance of tradition cannot be overstated. Traditions such as this distinguish us as a people; they bridge us to our rich and ancient heritage, they impart a sense of being. Along with our language, our age-old customs are our identifying marks. It is not an easy feat for this community to continue this tradition for the past one hundred years. The fact that we are celebrating the centennial of the grape blessing and festival speaks volumes about this community's love and reverence for our religious and national heritage and your commitment to carrying on the unique traditions that contribute to who we are."

Legend credits the ancient custom of Blessing of the Grapes to the Goddess of the Hearth, Astrik. As many pagan festivities were later adapted for Christian purposes, the Blessing's origins are found in ancient Armenia even before Armenia accepted Christianity as its official religion in 301 A.D. Religious texts record the bringing of first fruits, vegetables and nuts to the temple for blessing.

In their native land, the priest would lead a procession into the vineyard, carrying a cross in one hand, a pair of scissors in the other thanking God for the bounty of the harvest and beseeching him for his mercy in preserving the harvest from nature's destruction.

Church members are admonished to not eat any grapes until they have gathered at their churches to have the grapes blessed. Once the offerings have been blessed, the faithful each leave with a handful of grapes and go out into vineyards and private homes for their celebrations.

From the early custom of bringing produce, nuts, honey, bread and wine, to the temple for blessing, the Christian apostolic order changed the blessing ritual to offer only the wine and bread to the priest, symbolic of the blood of Jesus and his body in commemorating His crucifixion.

Not only do Armenians acknowledge and celebrate religious symbolism as in the Crucifixion of Christ, but also symbolism derived from ancient mythology, such as the symbolism of the pomegranate. Armenian fairy tales handed down through the ages repeat a familiar tale of three pomegranates sent from heaven: one for the story-teller, one for the listener and one for the world.

The pomegranate also symbolizes fertility and good fortune. Traditional weddings might include the practice of a bride tossing a pomegranate down to the ground. As it breaks, the scattered seeds suggest the fruit of her offspring. A host might offer a pomegranate to guests as a blessing of good fortune. However, the pomegranate is perhaps best known as a symbol of rebirth and survival for the Armenian people after the Armenian Genocide of the 20th century.

Festivities such as the Blessing of the Grapes are replete with music, sometimes played on a "bugle" such as Saroyan illustrates in his work, *Fresno Stories, My Heart is in the Highlands*. The haunting tones and melodies suggest the tragedies of the Armenian story, from genocide to a lost homeland. The memories are preserved in the celebrations of traditional religious events and holidays. The women, their work finished for the day, dance and play games in bold colorful costumes.

Fresh produce brought in from the fields adorn the farmer's market, where the grape is celebrated as "the queen of all fruits." Indeed, Saroyan considered the Central Valley's fields of vineyards, bringing forth lush grapes to be the most excellent in the entire world. During one of his visits to Armenia, he gathered a handful of grapes, relishing in their flavor, but said, "These are good, but not as good as Fresno's."

The fertile soil of the valley was the bed of vine roots, the fountain where they drank. I remembered (in the fiction room) how when, as it sometimes happened, I clipped off a good twig, a twig which would have borne fruit, I would feel guilty of a spiritual misdemeanor and would therefore ask the vine, as one might ask a mother whose child one is unintentionally hurt, to forgive me....

Again the vines were green with foliage and all the Armenians were going in their automobiles to the vineyards and gathering the tenderest leaves for the spring feasts. The children, born in California, stood among the vines, plucking the young leaves, holding dozens of them in their hands, speaking in Armenian. The leaf of the vine is a food, and the taste is never to be forgotten, even by those who are not Armenians. To Armenians the taste is the very taste of Armenia, and by eating the food each spring all Armenians, wherever they may be, declare to God and Armenia that they have remained loyal. Gathering the leaves of the vine is no small matter, and it is not purely an affair of the table.

Big Valley Vineyard, *The Daring Young Man on the Flying Trapeze*

Saroyan also writes of the perseverance and indominatable spirit of the Armenian people,

I should like to see any power of the world destroy this race, this small tribe of unimportant people, whose wars have all been fought and lost, whose structures have crumbled, literature is unread, music is unheard, and prayers are no more answered. Go ahead, destroy Armenia. See if you can do it. Send them into the desert without bread or water. Burn their homes and churches. Then see if they will not laugh, sing and pray again. For when two of them meet anywhere in the world, see if they will not create a new Armenia."

The Armenian and the Armenian

The generous spirit of Armenians is legendary. Saroyan was known to drop in with no notice, sometimes just to break bread served with a cup of coffee. Other times, a full meal. This hospitality is inherent in Armenian culture.

You must remember always to give, of everything you have. You must give foolishly even. You must be extravagant. You must give to all who come into your life. Then nothing and no one shall have power to cheat you of anything, for if you give to a thief, he cannot steal from you, and he himself is then no longer a thief. And the more you give, the more you will have to give.

The Human Comedy

Perhaps the inherited literary genes of his father and his love of books gave Saroyan expression to record the Armenian story throughout his work. Although he shunned traditional education taught in his schools and preferred instead to "read around" books held in the public library, he earned literary success by writing prolifically of his life growing up in Fresno.

Later as he traveled throughout the world, spending time in San Francisco, Los Angeles, New York, London, Paris and Armenia, the themes of his Armenian heritage and early years continued to influence his writings.

In New York, Saroyan indulged in dining at an upscale restaurant called The Golden Horn. The restaurant boasted a reputation of the best Armenian cuisine in the country in the 1950s. But it also had no match in elegance as illustrated from a recently purchased menu.

Saroyan both lived in and visited San Francisco where he shared a deep friendship with his kinsman, George Mardikian, who owned the popular restaurant, Omar Khayyam's. It was through their friendship, Saroyan encouraged Mardikian to preserve his Armenian recipes in his book, *"Dinner at Omar Khayyam's."*

Whereas San Francisco, New York, London, Paris and Armenia all held court to William Saroyan, it was Fresno that always drew him back, to his heritage and his beginning.

Dividing his time in both Paris and Fresno, Saroyan returned to Fresno and writes in his memoir,

> *In 1963 I had done a lot of living and traveling, and I thought it would be pleasant to go back to my hometown, my birthplace, Fresno, and feel when I had been there long ago from*

1915 to 1926, in fact—ten years of very great importance in my life.

2729 West Griffith Way, Fresno, California, 1964,
Places Where I've Done Time

Saroyan purchased two houses side-by-side where he lived until his death May 18, 1981.

In keeping with his deep regard for his Armenian heritage, Saroyan requested that his burial be in Armenia and Fresno. Interred at the Armenian Ararat Cemetery, he leaves his readers with this quotation from *"The Time of Your Life"* etched on his tombstone:

"In the time of your life, live—so that in that wondrous time you shall not add to the misery and sorrow of the world, but shall smile to the infinite variety and mystery of it."

His words have become clichés of life. His readers grasp at their deeper meaning, to define and validate their own human condition and to understand the literary genius beneath the words.

It is within that context, *Breaking Bread with William Saroyan* offers his words and recipes taken from the culture of Saroyan's Armenian heritage.

Then came Fresno, the home cooking, the food of Armenia, the famous dishes of Bitlis. Well, of course you know there are several basic foods among the Armenians, as well as among the Turks, Kurds, Arabs, Persians, Greeks, Georgians, Rumanians, Bulgarians, and two or three dozen other tribes, all the way from the Black Sea to the Siberian shores of the Pacific: yogurt and pilaf, or sour milk and rice, for instance. There are small differences in how the stuff is made, but these two items are basic. If you make the yogurt out of goat's milk, you get a different yogurt than the more common yogurt of cow's milk. And so it is with the milk of other animals....

The Eaters, *Here Comes There Goes You Know Who*

Paying tribute to his mother's home cooking, Saroyan reminds us of the smells of the foods that gave him not only physical sustenance, but spiritual nourishment:

There were also the magnificent smells in the house in which one did one's early time: the very walls themselves, the people who lived in the house, and the things they cooked or baked: Armenian bread, for instance, in the three popular forms prepared by the Saroyan family: the round, wafer-thin flat-bread, the oval loaf bread only an inch or two thick, and the diamond-shaped little loaves of butter bread. There was also always the smell of various green things, or growing things – parsley, mint, basil, onions, bell peppers, tomatoes, cucumbers, and so on and so forth. All of these things were a part of the place, and very quickly a part of me.

Bitlis, Fresno, Los Angeles, 1926, *Places Where I've Done Time*

Armenian bread was baked all the time at my house, in all of its forms: the rolled out flatbread, thinner than cardboard, the loaves, called Bahgh-arch, and the various breads with a great deal of oil or fat of one kind or another in them, called Gah-tah.

Now, when it was a day for the baking of bread, my mother would be up very early to get to it. She could easily have got-ten up three hours later in the winter-time when there was no work at the fruit-packing houses, but she didn't feel bread was being baked unless you got up in the dark, at five, sum-mer or winter, and went to work. By the time the rest of us were up and ready for breakfast her work was finished and the house was full of the smell of freshly baked bread, and the whole pleasant warmth of it, as it had been for several hours, while we slept. When we sat down to eat, though, we got the real treat of Bread Baking Day. This is called Tazhah-hotz, or new bread, and this is how it is made.

Take a handful of the bread dough, flatten it to a thickness of a little under an inch, and drop it into a frying pan in which any kind of fat you use, or butter, is very hot. In a few min-utes one side will be a handsome golden brown. Turn it over until the other side is the same, about six minutes all told. Now, break the thing, open up a pretty good-sized piece, and into the opening stuff white Armenian cheese. Drink tea with it. Only tea. Cocoa or coffee or anything else would make a mess of it. Hot, sharp, brisk, weak tea, after the manner of all of the tea-drinking peoples, accepting the British, who re-gard tea is coffee, to which they add milk.

The Eaters, *Here Comes There Goes You Know Who*

In *Breaking Bread with William Saroyan*, friends, family and business associates reveal his favorite foods and share cherished memories. For instance, Saroyan specifically instructed his butcher, Ken Cowan, to pre-pare Keyma for him. Here, not only are strict tenets of preparation ad-hered to, eating the raw, freshly ground meat must be done in a consis-tent time frame.

He was always drawn to authentic Armenian dishes; his friends recall his choices such as "sheep's head" and "kufta" with humor and respect.

With the words Saroyan used to describe the importance of foods in his own life, the recipes extracted from the pages of authentic Armenian cuisine tantalize our senses, and inspire us to embark on new culinary adventures.

RECIPES

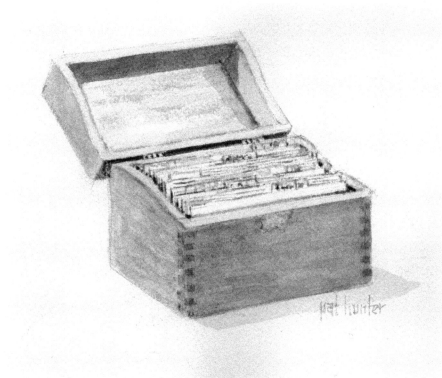

BREADS

Foreword to *Dinner at Omar Khayyam's*

By William Saroyan, San Francisco, California

When George Mardikian told me he was thinking of writing a cookbook, I knew it would be the most original one ever written, so I told him to be sure to go to work right away. I have never found it possible not to encourage any man who feels he has a book to write, let alone a great man like George. "Get that big frame of yours out of that kitchen," I told him, "and start writing." Now the book is written and I have given that the once over. Just as I thought, it is a prize package of a book, but it is more than a cookbook. It is the smiling chef himself — the generous-hearted, enthusiastic, easy-going George Mardikian himself talking to you just as he does in his famous restaurant, Omar Khayyam's; it is the big man with a bright face coming over to your table with a half-dozen out-of-the world dishes and telling you how they happened to come about in the great fable of man and hunger. It is the historian telling you history mingled skillfully with anecdotes from George's own beautiful fable. It is the comedian laughing with delight at the story of how he outwitted famine by inventing fabulous dishes from such lowly and abundant things as grain, water, salt, imagination and poetry. It is the man himself telling everybody how wonderful it is to be alive, and especially how wonderful it is to be alive in America. Naturally, I am delighted about George's book, just as I am always delighted with the food he serves and the manner in which he serves it. George Mardikian is the rarest chef in America — a man of exquisite good health, which spreads itself all around his restaurant like light from a walking human sun; a delightful wit with more stories than Omar himself; a continuous searcher for more and better table delights; a wise companion; and an eloquent speaker of both English and Armenian — my two favorite languages.

George is a countryman of mine, but that is not the only reason I am so fond of him — there are many countryman of mine whom I find it most difficult to cherish. I am fond of George because he is one of the most civilized human beings I have ever encountered. Because he has always been infinitely more than a guy in a kitchen preparing a supper for his friends and himself. Because he has never found it necessary to fuss too strenuously with the dull matters of making a profit and paying rent. Because his intention to make of his restaurants a civilized atmosphere for civilized people of all kinds has been more than realized. And because, in spite of all the demands on his time, he is never allowed himself to give anyone, however great or humble, the impression of being too busy to sit around and loaf. He is an excellent poker player and I have yet to see him lose without grace. He is interested in all good things and has yet to let a writer or a painter or a composer out of his restaurant without stuffing him with every kind of wonderful food in the place. On the other hand, he insists on feeding the lowly — he banquets newsboys as if they were the children of kings, and he fills his restaurant with homeless men as if they were the greatest men of our time....

I believe that anybody who owns this book is going to learn to make a good many dishes in his own kitchen; that he is going to appreciate good food more than ever; and that he is going to get more out of the experience of living.

Excerpt from *Dinner at Omar Khayyam's*
George Mardikian

Bread is the most important item in an Armenian's life, not only because he has been deprived of other foods for 600 years and has been compelled to thrive on bread, but also because it is considered a sacred product. No bread crumb falls to the ground in the presence of an Armenian, and goes unnoticed. He will immediately pick it up, kiss it, and say a prayer. Then he will place it on a wall for the birds to eat.

Breaking bread is a ceremonial custom, and a sign of hospitality in every Armenian household. And since every Armenian housewife must make her own bread, she has naturally found ways to shorten this daily labor. So, in years of experimenting, Armenian women have evolved lavash. This is a flat, round bread that can be kept a month without becoming moldy, and without losing its freshness. Although it looks like matzoth, it differs a great deal from them because lavash has both leavening and salt, while matzoth have neither. Lavash in Armenia is cooked in an oven in the ground or in the floor of the house. A pit is lined with bricks and the fire is laid directly on that. You must remove the coals before you put your bread in to bake. But in this country, with modern electrical and gas stoves, the operation is greatly simplified, so try the following recipe in your own oven.

LAVASH

Breads

Ingredients

3 pounds all-purpose flour

1 yeast cake

2 teaspoonfuls salt

lukewarm water to make a stiff dough

Directions

Dissolve yeast cake in 2 cups of warm water. Sift flour and salt into a large bowl. Make a depression in the center of the flour and gradually work in dissolved yeast cake and enough water to make a stiff dough. Knead well, place in bowl, cover, and let stand for about three hours. Punch dough down and let rise again.

Sift flour over a large board or table top, and spread evenly over surface. Now pinch off pieces of dough about the size of a large egg. With a long rolling pin (like a broomstick) roll dough out into a large sheet, as large as your oven will accommodate. Dough should be about 1/8-inch thick. Place on a cookie sheet, or the bottom of the oven, and bake at 400 degrees for about 3 minutes. Then place under broiler to brown the top lightly, watching all the time to keep from burning.

Repeat this process until all the dough has been used up. Store in a dry place and use as needed. To make sandwiches of lavash: Sprinkle water on both sides, and put in the desired filling. Then wrap in a towel for a few minutes before serving. Or spread the moistened lavash with a Bertouge cheese-and-parsley filling and roll up like Mexican tacos.

George Mardikian, *Dinner at Omar Khayyam's*

PEDA BREAD

Peda bread is the most popular Armenian bread in America. It is sold in all centers where Armenians gather. Peda, to me, tastes better during the Mohammedan Ramadan. That is the season when all Mohammedans observe 40 days of fasting during the hours when the sun is up. Even here in California I have had a chance to watch Egyptian and Arabian students from the International House in Berkeley enjoy breaking their fast. They fast all day, and then come to my restaurant to eat fresh peda bread and other native foods. This is the time when freshly baked peda bread tastes wonderful. It is sometimes called dunking bread, for it is so good when soaked up with meat and vegetable juices.

PEDA BREAD

Breads

Ingredients

6 cups flour

1 cupful milk or water

2 tablespoonfuls shortening or butter

1 tablespoonful salt

2 tablespoonfuls sugar

1 yeast cake

1/2 cupful lukewarm water

Directions

Dissolve yeast in lukewarm water. Warm the milk and add to it the sugar, melted shortening, and salt. Sift flour into a large bowl and work into it the liquids until it reaches the consistency of bread dough. Let rise, covered with a damp towel, for 2 hours. Remove to floured board and knead down. Cover again and let rise for about an hour.

Now pinch off pieces the size of a lemon. Roll out two oblong pieces 1/2-inch thick. Place side-by-side in a baking pan. You can make the loaves any size or shape you like, for individual or larger servings. Brush top of bread with butter. Bake in a 400 degree oven for 10 minutes, and then lower the heat to 350 degrees. Bake until nicely browned all over. Serve hot. This bread may be reheated in the oven for later use.

George Mardikian, *Dinner at Omar Khayyam's*

GATAH

Gatah is the favorite breakfast or tea bread. An Armenian may forget his mother tongue, he may forget everything about his native land, but he will never forget his mother's gatahs. In most cases, gatahs are like firm rolls sprinkled with sesame seed. They are delicious with tea, coffee or any hot beverage, and are especially recommended for afternoon snacks with cheese.

George Mardikian

HYASTANI GATAH

Breads

Ingredients

1 cupful pure melted butter

4 eggs

1 yeast cake

1 cupful sour cream or madzoon

1 teaspoon salt

9 cupfuls flour

3 cupfuls lukewarm water

1/2 cupful sesame seeds

Directions

Beat butter well until it is creamy. Add beaten eggs, and yeast that has been dissolved in warm water. Beat these well into the butter, then add sour cream

(or madzoon) and the salt. Mix well. Then gradually beat in flour and water to make a stiff dough. This mixing process should take about 15 minutes.

Now take a handful of dough and put it on a floured board or table. Beat the piece of dough against the table until it is very stringy, then place it in a large bowl. Repeat this until all the dough has been beaten. Then cover the bowl with a cloth and let the dough set until it rises—about 3 hours. To know the readiness of the dough you must recognize the aroma, or when you touch it with your hand it says, "I am ready."

When your gatah dough is ready, take out a piece about the size of a large apple. Roll it out very thin with your long rolling pin, as far as it will go without breaking. Brush it with melted butter or peanut oil. Fold up like a handkerchief into packages, brushing each fold with butter. In the last fold put 1/2 cupful of Khoridz stuffing. Make stuffing as follows:

STUFFING

Breads

Ingredients

1/2 cupful creamed butter

1 cupful sugar

3 cupfuls flour

Directions

Mix this together with your fingers until it is crumbly. Stuff into the folded dough. When packages are ready, flatten them out with a rolling pin to about 12 x 14 inches. They should be about 1- inch thick. Then cut them into any shape you like, say about 3-inch squares, or into oblong shapes. Set gatahs in a greased baking pan. Brush the tops with beaten egg yolks, and sprinkle with sesame seed. Bake in a pre-heated oven at 375 degrees for about 40 minutes.

George Mardikian, *Dinner at Omar Khayyam's*

I went around to the well and poured some cool water into a pitcher and took it to the old man. He drank the whole pitcherful in one long swig. Then he looked around the landscape and up at the sky and away up San Benito Avenue where the evening sun was beginning to go down. I reckon I'm five thousand miles from home, he said. Do you think we could eat a little bread and cheese to keep my body and spirit together?

The Man with the Heart in the Highlands, *Fresno Stories*

BREAKFAST FOODS

We ate mush in those days. It was cheap and we were poor, and the mush filled a lot of space. We used to buy it in bulk, by the pound, and we had it for breakfast every morning. There was a big bowl of it before me, about a pound and a half of it, steaming, and I began to swallow the food, feeling it sinking to my hunger, entering my blood, becoming myself in the change that was going on in me.

And Man, *The Daring Young Man on the Flying Trapeze*

EGGS

HAIGAGAN OMELETTE
Armenian Omelets

Breakfast Foods-Eggs

Ingredients

This is an excellent way to cook eggs when you wish to prepare a large quantity. Plan to use 1-1/2 eggs per person. To serve 4 people, use:

6 eggs

1 bell pepper

2 large fresh tomatoes, peeled and cut up

1/2 onion, chopped fine (optional)

1/4 pound boiled salami, chopped fine

1/2 cube butter

1/2 teaspoonful salt

Directions

Fry the finely chopped pepper and onion. Then add tomatoes and cook for 5 minutes. Add chopped salami, and heat thoroughly. Butter bottom of baking pan (a square cake pan is excellent). Beat the eggs and mix well with the tomato mixture. Bake in hot oven for 5 to 10 minutes, or until eggs are set and slightly brown on top. Cut in squares and serve immediately on very hot plates. This is a perfect dish for large parties or Sunday suppers. We serve it often for Armenian wedding breakfast in Fresno.

George Mardikian, *Dinner At Omar Khayyam's*

EGG AND CHEESE SOUFFLE

Breakfast Foods-Eggs

Ingredients

A Make-Ahead Dish for a Holiday Breakfast

10 slices white bread

1 pound lean bacon

3 tablespoons onion, minced

1 cup cheddar cheese, grated

1 cup jack cheese, grated

6 eggs, beaten well

3 cups milk

1/2 teaspoon salt

Directions

Butter a 9 inch by 13 inch Pyrex baking dish. Remove crusts from bread and cut into cubes. Fry, cool and crumble bacon. Mix together bread crumbs, bacon, onions, and cheeses, and put into the buttered baking dish. In a medium-sized bowl, mix the eggs, milk, and salt. Pour the egg mixture evenly over the ingredients in the baking dish. Cover with foil and chill overnight. Remove foil and bake in a 350 degree oven for 30 to 40 minutes. Cut and serve. Serves 12.

Mary Elia, *A Hundred Years and Still Cooking*

APPETIZERS

The creamery-faced girls with the creamery-bare arms stood behind the marble counter on which rested, always, four big glass pitchers of buttermilk. Real buttermilk, full of little specks of golden butter. On the counter were fresh, cool clean glasses.... There was a sign, which was hardly required: 'Fresh Buttermilk, All You Can Drink, 5 cents.'...

Danish Creamery, Fresno Street, Fresno, 1922,
Places Where I've Done Time

HUMMUS

Appetizers

Ingredients

2 16-ounce cans garbanzo beans
drained and rinsed

1/3 cup olive oil

4 tablespoons tahini

1 heaping teaspoon cumin

juice of 3 lemons

4-6 garlic cloves

Directions

Put all the ingredients in a food processor and blend for approximately 7 minutes until creamy. Spread in 9-inch round serving plate and sprinkle with cumin and crushed Syrian pepper. Cover and chill in refrigerator. You may drizzle with olive oil before serving. Serve with pocket bread, cracker bread, or with meat. Serves 6 to 8.

Karen Daoudian and Queenie Dardarian,
A Hundred Years and Still Cooking

YALANCHI

Appetizers

Ingredients

2 cups rice
1 cup oil
8 large onions, chopped fine
1 cup celery, chopped
1 8-ounce can tomato sauce
1/2 cup juice from dill pickles
1/2 cup lemon juice
1 bunch parsley, chopped
1 teaspoon dill weed
1/4 teaspoon allspice
cayenne pepper to taste
1 teaspoon paprika
1 tablespoon salt
grape leaves
2 tablespoons lemon juice
2 tablespoons oil

Directions

Cook onions and celery in the oil until tender. Add rice, lemon juice, dill weed, dill juice and can of tomato sauce. Cook for 10 minutes. Add chopped parsley and seasonings. Cool and roll in grape leaves.

Place in large pot and almost cover with boiling water. Cook on stove until it boils well. Then bake in oven at 325 degree for 45 minutes. Remove from oven and put 2 tablespoons lemon juice and 2 tablespoons oil over top and cover with leaves. Cool completely before removing from pan.

Katherine Karabian, *A Hundred Years and Still Cooking*

MISOV DEREVAPATAT
Stuffed Grape Leaves

Appetizers

Ingredients

This is another truly Armenian dish that should become a favorite with cooks in all parts of the country where grape leaves are obtainable. If they cannot be found in your locality, substitute cabbage or lettuce leaves.

1 pound ground shoulder of lamb

1/2 pound onions, chopped finely

2 tablespoonfuls chopped parsley

1/4 cupful rice

1 teaspoonful salt

black pepper to taste

juice of 1/2 lemon

1/3 cupful tomato purée

Directions

Boil grape leaves on until half cooked. Mix well all other ingredients and roll up in grape leaves in small packages about 3 inches long by 3/4 inch thick. Place in rows in a baking dish, and cover with water. Cover pan and bake in oven for 1 hour. Serve hot.

A delicious sauce is made by mixing madzoon with the gravy in which the grape leaves are cooked. Pour this over the grape leaves, to make a delicious and different light luncheon dish.

George Mardikian, *Dinner at Omar Khayyam's*

KEYMA

Appetizers

Ingredients

1- 2 pounds fresh, lean, round steak (purchase just prior to preparation)

Salt and pepper

1 cup (approx.) fine-ground bulgur soaked in equal parts of water for 2 hours or more

1/2 cup chopped parsley (Henry prefers the curly variety)

1/2 cup chopped green onions

Lemon and tomato juices (or tomato sauce) — amounts determined by absorption and texture

1 chopped tomato

Directions

Trim all fat and membranes from the meat. Grind the meat 3 times through the old-fashioned home-use meat grinder. (Consider using a food-processor with a meat-grind function.)

Salt and Pepper the ground meat.

Mix with bulgur (has been soaked, all liquid absorbed, bulgur is soft)

Add chopped parsley and green onions

Knead the meat, bulgur, parsley, and onions with tomato and lemon juices. Meat should be moist and hold together, but not be runny or overly wet.

Shape into small ping-pong ball size or sarma-size portions.

Serve immediately with Armenian cracker or peda bread as hors d'oeuvres or in a sandwich of peda bread.

Note: Keyma must be eaten within hours of purchase and preparation as it is a raw meat product. Keep refrigerated until the moment it is incorporated with the other ingredients. Do not freeze either the unground steak or ground keyma meat.

Remembered by Henry Eurgubian as told to his wife, Mary Eurgubian

To my amazement, when I first arrived in the United States I found that Americans knew very little about eggplant. The only way eggplant was served in restaurants or homes was the ordinary way of dipping it into batter and frying it most of the time. It was not even appetizing.

At my restaurant we serve it at least 120 different ways. I dare anyone to call me on that, because he will then be compelled to dine for 120 days at my place, and I will give him a different eggplant dish every day. There are probably hundreds of other ways to prepare it with which I am not familiar, but up to now I have had no difficulty in popularizing our eggplant specialties, which have become unusual delicacies. Dabgodz Sempoog is the type of appetizer that can be prepared in a short time and it can be preserved in the refrigerator for quite a few days. Now if you want to fry eggplant, try this method.

George Mardikian

DABGODZ SEMPOOG

Appetizers

Ingredients

2 large peeled, sliced eggplants

1 cup oil

2 cloves of garlic

1/2 cup of vinegar

Salt

Directions

Peel and slice eggplant. Salt well, and let it stand for 30 minutes. Heat oil in frying pan, add chopped garlic and sauté. Wash salted, sliced eggplant and dry on a towel. Then fry in oil to a golden brown color. Take out and set in deep dish. Pour vinegar over while hot, and let stand for 15 minutes. Drain off vinegar. Chill eggplant and serve as an appetizer or side vegetable dish.

As you will notice in the directions, I say salt the eggplant well. The purpose of this is to take the bitterness out. You can actually see the eggplant perspire.

George Mardikian, Dinner at Omar Khayyam's

43

EGGPLANT FRIED IN BATTER

Appetizers

Ingredients

1 large eggplant, unpeeled

3 large eggs

1/3 cup flour

1-1/2 cups corn or olive oil

Directions

Wash the eggplant, trim off the ends, and slice into 1-1/2 circles. Set aside Lightly beat the eggs in a mixing bowl and stir in the flour. Heat the oil in a heavy skillet over low heat. Drop the eggplant slices, one at a time, in the egg batter to completely coat both sides. Fry a few slices at a time in the hot oil until both sides are golden brown. Drain on paper towel. Keep hot. When all the eggplant is fried, arrange overlapping slices on a serving platter and serve as an accompaniment to sizzling grilled lamb chops and a garden fresh salad.

The Complete Armenian Cookbook

KHOROVADZ SEMPOOG AGHTZAN
Eggplant Caviar

Appetizers

Ingredients

1 eggplant

3 tomatoes

2 tablespoonfuls chopped onion

2 tablespoonfuls chopped parsley

3 tablespoonful vinegar

Salt and pepper

Directions

Bake or broil a whole large eggplant until soft. When broiled under open gas fire, it will burn outer skin, but eggplant will have a delicious smoked flavor. Let cool, then peel off browned or burned skin.

Chop moderately fine. Add chopped onions and parsley. Season with oil, vinegar, salt, pepper and mix well. Serve on lettuce leaf with olive in center; garnish with sliced tomato.

George Mardikian, *Dinner at Omar Khayyam's*

DABGADZ BASTEGH
Fried Bastegh and Egg

Appetizers

Ingredients

4 servings

1 egg

1/4 pound bastegh

butter

Directions

Beat the egg lightly. Cut the pieces of bastegh in half, and dip them into the beaten egg to coat both sides. Put 2 tablespoons butter in a skillet and add the pieces of egg-dipped basteghs. Cook the bastegh a minute or so on each side over a moderate flame, and remove to a serving plate. Continue cooking the balance, adding more butter as needed. Serve hot.

The Armenian Cookbook

SALADS

For me, though, the greatest meal in the whole world for a summer night was cold grapes, flat bread, white cheese, mint, bell peppers, green onions, tomatoes, cucumbers, and cold water.

The Millionaires, *Here Comes There Goes You Know Who*

Breaking Bread with William Saroyan

HAIGAGAN SALAD
Rudy Vallee Special

Salads

Ingredients

1 head of lettuce, cut in cubes

2 tomatoes, peeled and cut in eighths

1 cucumber, halved and sliced

1/2 cupful chopped parsley

1/3 cupful oil

1/3 cupful vinegar

salt and pepper

Directions

Mix cut vegetables lightly in bowl. Add salt, pepper, oil and vinegar. Toss to mix, and serve in attractive individual bowls, or on salad plates.

George Mardikian, *Dinner at Omar Khayyam's*

CELERY ROOT SALAD

Salads

Ingredients

2 large celery roots

1 onion, parsley, 2 bay leaves

salt and pepper

Directions

Peel celery root, and boil in a pot of stock or plain water to which cut-up onions, whole parsley, bay leaves, salt and pepper have been added. When tender, remove from pot and slice in small pieces, as in potato salad. Serve with this dressing:

1 cupful oil (oil or peanut)
1 cupful vinegar (tarragon)
1/3 teaspoonful mustard
1/2 teaspoonful salt
1/4 teaspoonful freshly ground black pepper

Mix all together and pour over sliced celery root while it is still hot, so that dressing will soak into vegetable. Chill and serve on lettuce leaves.

George Mardikian, Dinner at Omar Khayyam's

ROMAINE SALAD A LA OMAR

Salads

Ingredients

2 heads romaine lettuce

1/2 cupful mayonnaise

1/2 cup full catsup

2 tablespoonfuls vinegar

1 teaspoonful Worcestershire sauce

1/2 teaspoonfuls salt

dash of pepper

1 chopped hard boiled egg

Directions

Lay romaine leaves on flat salad plates. Mix mayonnaise, adding balance of ingredients, into a smooth dressing. Pour over romaine and sprinkle top with chopped eggs and paprika. Serve.

George Mardikian, *Dinner at Omar Khayyam's*

TABBOULEH SALAD

Salads

Ingredients

1/2 cup fine (# grade) bulgur
6 ripe tomatoes, minced
1 small onion, minced
6 green onions minced
1 bunch parsley, minced
1/2 bunch fresh mint, minced
3 cucumbers, diced (optional)

Dressing
1 cup light olive oil
1 cup lemon juice
salt and hot red pepper to taste
pinch of black pepper
romaine lettuce leaves for garnish.

Directions

In a mixing bowl combine the bulgur and the tomatoes with their juice. Let it stay at room temperature for about 30 to 60 minutes until the bulgur is soft and the tomato liquid absorbed. Add all the other vegetables and mix gently but thoroughly. Combine the dressing ingredients in a separate bowl and pour over the bulgur mixture. Mix well. Chill. Serve in a wooden salad bowl, well chilled, and surrounded with romaine lettuce leaves for garnish.

The Complete Armenian Cookbook

SWISS CHARD SALAD
(Armenian)

Salads

Ingredients

2 bunches Swiss chard

1/4 cup tahini

9 tablespoons lemon juice

3 cloves garlic, pressed

1 cup cold water

salt and hot red pepper to taste

1 can (8 ounces) tomato sauce

1 bunch parsley, minced

1 bunch green onions, minced

Directions

Wash the Swiss chard thoroughly under running cold water, remove stems and chop. Place in a saucepan with water to cover. Bring to a boil over high heat, reduce heat and simmer about 15 minutes. Drain. Squeeze out the excess water. Set aside.

In a mixing bowl, combine the tahini, lemon juice, garlic, water, salt and red pepper. Blend well.

Combine Swiss chard with the tahini mixture, tomato sauce, parsley and onion. Mix well. Chill. This tangy salad is excellent with lentil kufte.

The Complete Armenian Cookbook

BABA GHANOUSH

Salads

Ingredients

Eggplant salad
4 servings
1 large eggplant
1 large tomato
1 small onion, finely chopped
1 small green pepper, finely chopped
1/2 cup parsley, finely chopped
1-1/2 teaspoons salt
1-1/2 teaspoons vinegar
4 teaspoons olive oil

Directions

Wash the eggplant, place it in a baking dish and put under the broiler. When the skin of the eggplant facing the flame becomes charred, turn it, and continue until all sides are well charred. Remove the pan and set aside.

When the eggplant is cool enough to handle, slit the top, scoop out the pulp with the spoon, and place it into a bowl. Discard the skin. Chop the pulp with a knife until it is partially mashed. Cut the tomato into small pieces, and add it to the eggplant with the chopped onion, green pepper, and parsley. Add the salt, vinegar and olive oil, and mix well. Chill.

The Armenian Cookbook

VEGETABLE DISHES

After we had set up the stand, and had put boxes of fruit and vegetables on display, Ahboud handed me a cloth and asked me to shine the oranges. He watched me quickly transform a dusty orange into a sparkling jewel, nodded, and himself worked at more difficult or complicated problems — he had six boxes of tomatoes in which some were becoming oversoft. These he carefully removed to a separate box, and later offered them to some old ladies who came by, for almost nothing — six or seven pounds for a nickel, for instance. They knew what to do with such tomatoes. They knew that such tomatoes were the best for their purposes. They made a concentration of them, called salsa, which served them during the winter.

Ahboud's Stand at the Fresno Free Market, 1917,
Places Where I've Done Time

One of the staple vegetables of Armenia is eggplant, and I hope someday it will be a favorite in this country, too. It is so easily raised, so easily kept, and so easily cooked when you know how.

Our chief eggplant delicacy is a dish called Imam Bayeldi, which literally means "the priest fainted." ... I have often served this dish at gourmet dinners and I have never seen anyone who hasn't been enthusiastic about it. It is the favorite dish of Alfred Lunt and Lynn Fontanne. This is how you make it.

George Mardikian

IMAM BAYELDI

Vegetables

Ingredients

2 large eggplants

1 pound onions, sliced

1/2 pound green peppers

1/2 cupful chopped parsley

1 cupful olive or peanut oil

1 pound tomatoes, or 1 No. 2 can solid pack tomatoes

Directions

Cut the eggplants into quarters, 8 pieces all together. Salt them and let them stand until they start to perspire. Dark water will ooze out of the pieces. Meanwhile, prepare the stuffing:

Slice onion and peppers and sauté gently in the oil. Just about the time these are soft, add tomatoes, parsley, salt and pepper and cook for 2 minutes.

Wash eggplant, make a slit down the center of each segment and stuff with the cooked vegetable combination. Add 2 cups of water, and bake in the oven for 1 hour.

George Mardikian, *Dinner at Omar Khayyam's*

pat hunter

MANTI (PASTE)

Manti is an Armenian version of an original paste. Since Armenians love to be first, I suspect they were annoyed to find that the Chinese were the discoverers of macaroni, and through Marco Polo paste was first introduced to the near East. Armenians tried to make something new of it after it was introduced to them, and manti is the result. It must be served with madzoon.

This is where the Armenian in me enters the picture, because for this dish I use a lot of garlic.

The dough is the same as the Sou Beurek dough, but you roll it out 1/16-inch thick. Then cut into 1-inch squares. Add 1/4 teaspoonful of stuffing and fold into a package, pressing the edges of the dough together. Grease a baking pan and place the package in it, rather close together. Bake in a hot oven until light brown. Drain off the butter that might have accumulated and pour well-seasoned chicken or turkey broth over the squares, adding enough to cover. Bake again for another 20 minutes. Serve hot. These should be served with madzoon seasoned with garlic.

George Mardikian

STUFFING

Vegetables

Ingredients

1/2 pound lean lamb ground

1 small onion chopped fine

salt and pepper

Directions

Cook together in butter until done. Let it get cold before stuffing manti.

MANTI SPINACH PASTE

Vegetables

Ingredients

Follow directions for Banirov Beurek using chopped spinach. We usually add a little cheese to kill the flatness of the spinach, or if you don't care for this combination, braised browned meat and spinach make an interesting combination.

Spinach stuffing:

Salt raw spinach leaves and let stand for 1 hour. Squeeze the spinach to soften it, and wash with cold water. Sauté in butter; add salt, pepper, and cheese, and use as stuffing.

Macaroni cheese paste:

This is a dish for all who are in a hurry who like macaroni and who don't mind the calories. Get very thick macaroni of the seashell variety. Boil it for about 12 minutes in salted water. Take out and drain well. Butter a baking pan,

Directions

and put in it alternately a thin layer of macaroni, then a thick layer of grated cheese mixed with chopped parsley and beaten egg. When you have used up all the macaroni, put lots more cheese on top, sprinkle with paprika, and bake in a hot oven for 15 minutes. If you are making this dish or more than 4 people use 2 beaten eggs.

George Mardikian, *Dinner at Omar Khayyam's*

MANTI
Meat filled pastry boats baked and served with madzoon; 6 servings

Vegetables

Ingredients

1 pound chopped lamb

1 onion, finely chopped

2 tablespoons parsley finely chopped

1-1/2 teaspoons salt

1/8 teaspoon pepper

3-1/4 cups flour

1 egg

2 tablespoons melted butter

1 cup warm water

1/8 pound melted butter

6 cups chicken broth

madzoon

Directions

Combine the meat with onion, parsley, 1 teaspoon salt, and pepper. Mix thoroughly and set aside.

Combine the flour, 1/2 teaspoon salt, egg, 2 tablespoons melted butter and the warm water in a mixing bowl. Knead the dough until it is smooth. Divide the dough into two balls and cover them with a towel to keep them warm. Let them rest for 1/2 hour.

Take a rolling pin and roll each ball of dough to a thickness of 1/8 inch. Cut the rolled dough into 1-1/2 inch squares and fill each square with a small amount of the meat mixture (about the size of a marble). Pinch the two ends of the dough together to resemble a boat. Continue making the boats until all of the dough has been used. Put the 1/8 - pound of melted butter in a baking pan, and arrange the filled boats (manti) in the pan, one next to another.

Bake at 375 degrees for 1/2 hour or until the manti is lightly browned. Add the hot chicken broth to the pan and bake for 5 minutes longer.

Serve in individual dishes with a little of the broth. Add 2 or 3 table-spoons of madzoon to the center of each serving.

The Armenian Cookbook

MEATS

Also, common to all of these people is lamb roasted on skewers over a no-longer flaming fire or shish-kebab. Shish is Turkish for spear and kebab is Turkish for cut-up lamb. Tass-kebab would therefore be cut-up lamb cooked in a tass or pan. And so on. On a spear it would go like this, more or less, for flavor and variety: a piece of meat, a piece of bell pepper, onion, tomato, and then another piece of meat, and so on, depending on what you had plentiest of. And so that sort of eating was routine for me in Fresno, excepting the shish-kebab, which had to wait for a family picnic, or a whole big Armenian picnic, because you had to prepare it right if you really wanted it to be what it ought to be.

The Eaters, *Here Comes There Goes You Know Who*

Lamb is the staple meat of the Near East. There are more ways of preparing it than any other kind of meat. I say this as an authority, not because I know more ways to cook lamb than any other cook in the world, but because I have traveled all over this globe and seen it done. It is unfortunate that in America we know so little about lamb. The fault does not lie with the housewife or average restaurateur, but with the growers and the butchers who have failed to educate consumers in ways to use all cuts of the animal.

There is, as you know, a great deal of difference between lamb and mutton. In the past, we have had no way of preventing the butcher or the restaurateur from selling mutton when lamb is requested. Hence a prejudice has arisen against it.

Lamb is the traditional ceremonial food in Armenia, as turkey is in America. Armenians roast lamb on their memorial days, or *Madagh*. People go to the churchyards for prayer, then afterwards they give the poor and needy a wonderful feast of roast lamb with pilaff.

I remember my first impression of the mountain folk in the Caucasus at the time when I marched over the rocky roads to get to Karabagh. In this remote country they have no inns such as you find in the lower plateaus. You automatically become the guest of the *melik*, or *keghia*, and who is the mayor, the judge, the chief of police, and host par excellence. When you enter his home the daughter of the household, or the wife, brings a basin of water and you wash your feet. There could be no greater courtesy for you have marched over sharp stones and rough vegetation, and probably your feet are sore and bleeding. Then you are presented with a brand-new pair of woolen socks woven by members of the household from wool spun by the womenfolk. They take away your soiled socks, and when you are ready to leave you find them with your belongings, mended and clean.

If you are a person of consequence, you become the guest of the whole village. You stand at evening in front of the *melik's* house, and everybody comes by to shake hands with you. At sundown you hear the bells of the flocks of sheep coming in. As they pass, the *melik* and some of the elders pick out the best horned ram in the flock, and the sheep-herder drives the rest of the flock home.

Then he returns and starts carving the ram, which has been slaughtered. Through my profession and travels I have seen many master butchers and chefs who know how to handle a knife. But never have I seen anything like the skill of a shepherd of the Caucasian mountains when it comes to skinning a lamb from an opening in the neck of not more than 6 or 8 inches. With a single sharp-edged knife, he slits the skin of the animal, then pulls the body of the lamb from that little opening. He then removes the intestines, takes the lamb to the spring, and washes it thoroughly. He stuffs the cavity with pilaff dressing, sews it up, seasons it well, and then puts it back into the skin.

The lamb is then placed in a prepared pit. It is about 5 feet deep, and leaves are placed in the bottom. The lamb is covered with about 4 inches of dirt, so that the fire doesn't touch the skin. Then burning logs are put over it — enough to burn most of the night — and while this is flaming and sparkling the villagers make merry. Everybody turns out, including musicians and *ashoughs*, who are like our minstrels.

But the day of all days is the following one. The lamb is taken out of the pit and put on a huge table. The priest of the village blesses it. The man who is to carve the lamb waits until everybody holds a candle that is been made from beeswax by the priest himself. Our host, the *melik*, takes a light from the priest and carries it over to the guest of honor, who is the only person in the congregation who has a right to light more than one candle. The guest then lights the candle of his neighbor to the right and left, and so it is passed around. Not until then is the lamb carved. I challenge anyone who has partaken of this to name a dish that tastes more delicious.

When the skin is removed from the roasted lamb, you see the juiciest meat imaginable. But the juice disappears rapidly, because everybody has provided himself with a hunk of bread and is ready to reach over and dunk in it. Then he waits for his pilaff and piece of meat. And here one custom, originating long before Christ, still exists. You eat with your hands, for the use of knives and forks is taboo.

George Mardikian, *Dinner at Omar Khayyman's*

SHISH KEBAB

Naturally a whole roast lamb cannot be served on every ceremonial occasion. So shish kebab or *khorovadz* has been evolved. This is to Armenians what corned beef and cabbage is to the Irish. It is like the Russian *shaslik*. The history of *shashlik* dates far back, but the known origin can be traced to the mountain folk of the Caucasus who, during their migrations, would kill wild game, stick it on their swords, and roast it over the fire. Hence the name shish kebab, which means barbecue or skewer for which the sword served.

All during the years we have served shish kebab, this has been one of our most popular dishes. It is made of lamb seasoned in sherry, onion and oregano, an herb that grows in all the Mediterranean countries. The combination of these three gives a flavor similar to garlic but with none of the aftertaste. Always serve shish kebab with pilaff.

SHISH KEBAB

Meats

Ingredients

To make shish kebab use:

1 leg of lamb (5 or 6 pounds)

1/2 pound onions

1 tablespoon salt

1/2 teaspoonful pepper

1/3 cup sherry

2 tablespoonfuls oil

1 teaspoonful oregano

Directions

Remove all fat and gristle from the leg of lamb. Bone it and cut into 1-inch squares. Mix meat with sliced onions, seasonings and other ingredients. Let meat marinate in sauce at least an hour, and preferably overnight. Put on skewers and broil over charcoal fire or gas broiler until crisply brown on all sides.

George Mardikian, *Dinner at Omar Khayyam's*

KOUZOU KZARTMA
Roast shank of Lamb

Meats

Ingredients

4 shanks of lamb

4 large pieces of potato

2 tomatoes, quartered

2 teaspoonfuls salt

1 teaspoonful paprika

2 cupfuls water

Directions

Wash lamb well and let it stand in clean water for at least 15 minutes. Place in open roasting pan; add tomatoes, salt, paprika, and water. Cook for 30minutes at 375 degrees, turn meat over and cook for another 30 minutes. Now add potatoes to same pan and roast with the shanks for 30 minutes, then turn both potatoes and meat and let cook for another 30 minutes. Meat should cook for 2 hours altogether. Serve with its own juice as gravy.

George Mardikian, *Dinner at Omar Khayyam's*

LAMB LOIN ROAST
(Armenian)

Meats

Ingredients

1 lamb loin roast, 3 pounds
salt and pepper
1 cup blue rose rice
1 cup ground beef or lamb
1/2 cup pine nuts
1/4 cup sliced almonds
1 teaspoon salt
1/2 teaspoon black pepper
1/2 teaspoon allspice
1/4 teaspoon cinnamon
1/8 teaspoon cloves

Cooking ingredients:
water
1 inch cinnamon stick
8 whole peppercorns
4 whole cloves

Directions

4 whole allspice
3 bay leaves
1 cup yogurt

When you buy the meat, have your butcher cut a pocket in the lamb roast. Sprinkle the outside and inside of the roast with salt and pepper. Set aside.

Soak the rice with cold, salty water. Set aside.

Meanwhile, prepare the filling by combining the ground meat, nuts and spices. Stir in the washed rice, mixing well. Fill the pocket with the stuffing. Skewer the pocket shut or sew with a large needle and thread. Place the roast in a large heavy pan. Cover with water and add the remaining cooking ingredients. Cover with lid. Bring to boil over high heat. Reduce heat and simmer 1 hour. Drain the liquid. Transfer the lamb to a lightly greased roasting pan. Spread the yogurt evenly over the meat and roast at 350 degrees about 30 minutes or until nicely browned.

The Armenian Cookbook

LAMB SHANKS
Serve with Pilav

Meats

Ingredients

6 lamb shanks
2 large onions, sliced
3 cloves garlic
1 large bell pepper, sliced
1 large can tomatoes
1/4 cup brown sugar
2 cups water
4 teaspoons dry mustard
2 teaspoons salt
1/2 cup vinegar
1 cup catsup
1/2 cup oil
3 teaspoons Worcestershire sauce.

Directions

Brown the lamb shanks by putting them in a 450-degree oven in oil. In a large bowl, combine the onions, garlic, pepper, tomatoes, brown sugar, water, dry mustard, salt, vinegar, catsup and Worcestershire sauce. Pour over the browned lamb, cover and bake for 1-1/2 hours at 350 degrees. Uncover and bake for 1/2 hour longer. Baste often while cooking. Serves 6. Enjoy!

Mary Elia, *A Hundred Years and Still Cooking*

The wheat that was cracked small was mixed with ground meat to make meatballs of all kinds, solid, or with a stuffing made of pomegranate seeds, or to stuff into tomatoes, bell peppers, squash, zucchini, pumpkin, eggplant, and to wrap grape leaves around it. In Armenia they stuff apples and quince, too, but that wasn't anything that was done in my house. Dried apricots and peaches went into thick meaty stews to cut the heavy flavor of the meat and garlic and dried eggplant and okra and whatever else might be in there, but apples and quince were not used in that way. They could be, of course. The best cooking comes from necessity. You use what you have and you find out how to use it well.

The Eaters, *Here Comes There Goes You Know Who*

pat hunter

KUFTÉ

Kuftés are used in Armenia for basic quick dinners. All are made with ground meat, the most popular one being Izmir Kufté, which means meatball of Smyrna.

It is a glorified hamburger, given a nice Near Eastern touch by the addition of cumin (spice) and a good bit of parsley and onion. Kufté can be made with any kind of ground meat, or a mixture of several kinds.

George Mardikian

IZMIR KUFTÉ

Kuftés

Ingredients

1 pound ground meat

1 raw egg

1/2 cupful finely chopped onion

1/4 cupful very finely chopped parsley

1 cupful soaked bread or toasted crumbs

1/2 teaspoonful cumin

salt and pepper

Directions

Mix all ingredients together, and form into thumb-shaped patties. Fry in butter if you are in a hurry, but they are more delicious if baked in a well-buttered pan in a very hot oven. Serve with pilaff.

George Mardikian, *Dinner at Omar Khayyam's*

HARPUT KUFTÉ

Kuftés

Ingredients

This kufté is most popular in America — in fact, it is more popular here than in Armenia. The reason is that most of the Armenians in this country come from Harput, where the first American missionaries were established. Here was built the Euphrates American College, which had a great deal to do with starting the Armenian migration to America.

Harout kufté is a stuffed meatball, and it may be served either with its broth or dry.

1 pound ground lean beef or lamb

1 cupful very fine bulgur (cracked wheat)

salt and pepper

Directions

To prepare kufté, mix meat and cbulgur with salt and pepper. Kneed for 15 minutes until blended into a gummy mixture. Make into balls the size of a walnut by rolling in the palm of hand. With the thumb, make a hollow in each ball to hold the stuffing and press the side walls thin. Slip in stuffing and press top of ball closed, smoothing the place and sealing it by rolling ball between the palms. Stuffed balls are then dropped into boiling seasoned soup stock which has been cooking for 1 hour with 1/4 cupful chopped parsley, 1/2 cupful onion, and 1 cup tomatoes. When the kuftés are cooked, they will rise to the surface. This will take about 20 minutes. Do not cook too many in the pot at one time, since they require room to rise.

Remove from soup stock. If kuftés are to be served dry, heat in butter in the oven to make a crisp crust. Or they may be served with soup stock in deep bowls. Try not to break the surface of the balls when removing them from soup stock, or you will lose some of the spicy juices that have been sealed inside.

STUFFING

Kuftés

Ingredients

1 large sliced onion

1 cube butter or 1/2 cupful

2 tablespoonfuls pine nuts

2 tablespoonfuls chopped parsley

1/4 teaspoonful allspice

1/4 teaspoonful ground cinnamon

2 tablespoonfuls currants (optional)

Directions

To prepare stuffing, fry onion in butter to the stage just before it turns pink, or, as Armenians say, until it is well-killed. Add parsley and other ingredients and cook together for 5 minutes. Put in a dish and chill in refrigerator. When chilled, make into a ball the size of a large marble, and insert this into hollow of meatball.

George Mardikian, *Dinner at Omar Khayyam's*

MEAT COOKED WITH VEGETABLES

My mother was partial to vegetables, and she was a typical, average Armenian housekeeper. The method I am now going to suggest, therefore, isn't my invention. It represents centuries of trial and error in bringing out the best in vegetables to please generations of gourmets. . . .

Armenians are very partial to baking foods instead of frying them. I have always claimed that one of the worst enemies of American health has been the frying pan. Proof? Take your frying pan and fry a couple of fresh tomatoes and butter. Then break in a couple of eggs (so that you won't waste the butter and tomatoes). This will make a good breakfast. But note the difference in the pan when you have taken the food out. The frying pan will be all shined up, but the tomatoes and eggs will have picked up all the flavors and discoloration from the pan.

These meat and vegetable recipes aim, by baking and proper cooking, to preserve every unit of all the vitamins, and so contribute to the health of the nation.

We will start off with a series of *misovs*; *misov* means with meat.

MISOV PAGLA
Fresh Fava or Horse Beans

Meat with Vegetables

Ingredients

1 pound shoulder of lamb, cut up for stew

1 cupful sliced onions

2 pounds tender, stringless fava beans

2 tablespoons chopped fresh dill

salt and pepper

water

Directions

Braise meat until nicely browned; add onions and cook for 15 minutes. Cut up fava beans into lengths as you would string beans. Add dill seasoning, salt and pepper, and water to half cover. Put on lid and bake or steam onto tender.

George Mardikian, *Dinner at Omar Khayyam's*

PACHA

A special lamb stew prepared with lamb tongues and calves' feet, 6 servings

Meat with Vegetables

Ingredients

4 calves' feet

2 cloves garlic

salt and pepper to taste

6 lamb tongues

Directions

Singe and scrape the calves' feet to be sure they are clean. Wash them thoroughly, and place them in a large kettle, with water to cover. Bring the mixture to a boil, and lower the flame to let it simmer. Remove the scum from time to time.

Add the garlic, salt and pepper, and cook for about 5 hours. Trim and wash the tongues. Place them in a saucepan, with water to cover, and salt to taste. Cook the tongues until they are tender. Drain the water and remove the skin from the tongues, while they are still hot. Add the peeled tongues to the kettle and cook for 1 hour longer. Remove all the bones. Serve in soup bowls as a main course.

The Armenian Cookbook

LAMB'S HEAD SOUP

Meat with Vegetables

Ingredients

1-2 lamb's heads
4 medium size carrots
5 stocks celery
1 bell pepper (Green)
2 medium size onions,
    yellow or brown
2 cloves garlic
1 tablespoon tomato paste
1 full can refried beans (15oz.),
    for thickening the soup
1 full can chopped petite tomatoes
    (15 oz.)
2 teaspoons oregano
1 teaspoon thyme
1 whole bay leaf
2 tablespoons Worcestershire sauce
1 teaspoon soy sauce

Directions

3 tablespoons olive oil
2 tablespoons parsley, chopped into soup
    and 1-2 tablespoons for garnish
1 teaspoon black pepper
1/2 teaspoon salt

Chop all of the vegetables into bite-size pieces.

Smash garlic and then chop.

In large deep pan, heat the olive oil using medium level heat.

Place the garlic and onions in the heated olive oil and soften.

Place all remaining vegetables into the same large deep pan, and sauté the ingredients, stirring often to prevent burning

Cook until soft, about 15-**20 minutes**

Add 3 quarts of water to the sautéed vegetables cooking in the large deep pan.

LAMB'S HEAD SOUP
(Continued)

Meat with Vegetables

Ingredients

Directions

Add all remaining spices –tomato paste, refried beans, chopped petite tomatoes, oregano, thyme, bay leaf, Worcestershire sauce, soy sauce, black pepper and salt.

Add the washed lamb's heads into the mixture.

Bring the contents to a boil, place a lid (cover) over the pan, reduce the heat to a simmer, and cook for 1-1/2 to 2 hours. Note: When the meat starts falling off of the bone of the lamb's head, this indicates that the cooking is complete.

Remove lamb's heads, and separate the meat from the bones, and dispose of bones.

Add the separated meat back into the large deep pan cooking the vegetables.

Add the parsley garnish atop the finished soup presentation.

Note: *The refried beans are used as a thickening agent for the soup. To eliminate the look of the skins in the paste, run the full can of ingredients through a blender or food processer. If desired, substitute a flour/butter mixture for thickening. However, the refried beans give the soup a very even, consistent thickness.

Frances Radoicich

MISOV GANANCH LOBIA
String Bean Stew

Meat with Vegetables

Ingredients

1 pound shoulder of lamb cut for stew

1 cupful sliced onions

2 pounds string beans

1 cupful fresh or canned tomatoes

salt and pepper

3 cupfuls water

Directions

Braise meat until brown; add onions and cook for 15 minutes. Cut string beans lengthwise and add to meat. Pour over tomatoes and water, salt and pepper, and bake covered until tender. Or you may steam this stew on top of the stove, if tightly covered.

George Mardikian, Dinner at Omar Khayyam's

MISOV SEMPOOG
Eggplant Stew

Meat with Vegetables

Ingredients

1 pound shoulder of lamb cut for stew

2 pounds eggplant

1/2 pound onions sliced (about one cupful)

1/2 pound fresh tomatoes or one cupful canned

salt and pepper

1 teaspoonful paprika

3 cupfuls water

Directions

Braise meat until brown; add onions and braise with meat until soft. Cut eggplant into 2-inch cubes, and add to meat mixture. Pour over tomatoes, salt, pepper, paprika and water, and bake for 1 hour.

George Mardikian, *Dinner at Omar Khayyam's*

The favorite dish at my house is what the people of Bitlis call Tut-too. Perhaps that isn't the spelling likeliest to help you get the pronunciation of it, but it's said swiftly, with the accent on the last syllable. There is almost no first syllable, actually. The word means sour, or tart. Take a big cabbage, cut it up big or small or both, put it in a crock, throw some salt in there, a piece of bread, or a little dry yeast, pour warm water over the stuff until the water is near the top of the crock, then place a dish over the stuff, and place a weight on the dish to press the solid stuff down. We always used a rock about the size of a big eggplant. After seven, eight, or nine days the stuff is sharp, it has gone sour, but nothing like sauerkraut, something else, in my opinion something much better. The juice deeply satisfies thirst, and is considered an invigorating tonic. Now, if you have other stuff, put other stuff in there with the cut-up cabbage, too: turnip greens especially celery, green tomatoes, and all like that. It's good raw, the juice is always good cold, but the stuff is prepared pretty much with the intention of cooking this great dish I am speaking of: Tut-too.

In my family there were only five of us, but two of us were very good eaters, that is, my brother and myself, so my mother used a large pot, three gallons or more. First, she put a gallon of the sour juice in there, and half a gallon of water because that much of the liquid would boil away in the cooking. Into the juice, she dumped three or four pounds of cut-up shoulder of lamb, bone and all. When the lamb had cooked *for half an hour or so, or a little less, she added three or four pounds of the sour cabbage, and a cup of washed **gorgote**: well, **gorgote** might be barley, but I'm not sure. It cooks in there, opens up, and is a very important part of the dish. It **ought** to be in there. Then six or seven big tomatoes are cut up and put in there, and after the whole thing has stewed for an hour or more you have got it. If there is any left over, it is always better the second day. It is eaten steaming hot. In the winter it is great.*

The Eaters, *Here Comes There Goes You Know Who*

BITLIS TUTOO
Sour Cabbage Stew

Meat with Vegetables

Ingredients

Tutoo is a dish that comes from the people of Bitlis and Moosh in Western Armenia. It is thought by some historians to be a very old recipe brought by the French Crusaders, who married Armenian girls and stayed in the Bitlis area.

1 pound lamb necks or stew meat

1-2 large onions, chopped

8 cups fermented cabbage
   with its own juice

3/4 cup dzedzads (whole wheat gorghod)

1 8-ounce can tomato sauce

1 can water

Juice of one lemon
   (add more for tart flavor)

Directions

To Ferment Cabbage:

3 large heads cabbage chopped in 1 inch squares pickling salt
   not iodized

1/4 cup dzedzads (whole wheat gorghod)

4 quarts of water

In a large kettle, cover the meat with cabbage water and cook for 1/2 hour. Add onions, cabbage, dzedzads, tomato sauce, 1 can water and lemon juice, then cook slowly for another hour or until meat is done.

(Have ready a large crock for fermenting cabbage.) Bring water to a boil and add salt to taste. Let it cool to tepid temperature. Pour water over cut cabbages to cover top. Cover container partially, leaving an opening for stirring. Stir thoroughly to help release gases caused by fermentation once or twice a day for 1 week to 10 days. After cabbage has fermented, refrigerate tutoo by transferring it to large glass jars or other containers. Serves 6.

Queenie Dardarian, *A Hundred Years and Still Cooking*

NANNY'S CABBAGE SOUP

Meat with Vegetables

Ingredients

1/2 cabbage chopped small

1 big yellow onion, chopped

Start it in 1/4 cup oil in the pan and
   add a can of tomato sauce or can of
   chopped tomatoes

2 or 3 carrots, chopped

2 or 3 pieces of celery

1/2 cup parsley

2 heaping spoonfuls of barley

Throw in a handful of noodles
   (any kind you want to get rid of)

2 cans of chicken broth (if you need
   more water, add a couple of glasses)

And any vegetable in the crisper you
   need to get rid of. (I threw in a
   chopped potato at the last minute.)

Salt and pepper to taste.

Directions

I also had some frozen chicken meat in the freezer and I threw that in, plus some lemon juice. If you want, you can add anything in this soup, and be happy with the taste. On a day that is cold outside, it's really delicious.

Hope you enjoy this recipe. I made it up, and on days when I don't want to cook, I take a carton that I have frozen and have it for lunch.

Virginia Derian

MISOV BAMIA
Okra with Meat

Meat with Vegetables

Ingredients

1 pound shoulder of lamb, cut for stew

1 large onion, sliced

1 pound okra

1/2 pound tomatoes cut up

1 whole lemon

salt and pepper

3 cupfuls water

Directions

Braise meat until brown; add onions and cook for 10 minutes. To prepare okra, remove stems without making an opening in the end of the pods. This will prevent the sticky juice from running out and will make the stew more palatable. Add okra to meat mixture. Prick holes in a whole lemon with a fork, and drop this in with the okra. This will counteract the juices of the okra, to which some people object. Add also the tomatoes, salt, pepper and water. Cook for 1 hour tightly covered.

You may use young green grapes instead of the lemon for keeping the okra crisp and whole. Note: Get medium-sized okra, and you will find it is more delicate in flavor.

George Mardikian, Dinner at Omar Khayyam's

KEBA

The combination of lamb, bulgur, and fresh produce from the garden are found in many Armenian recipes. This Keba recipe from the kitchen of Ruth Elia is one delicious way to prepare these tasty foods.

CRACKED WHEAT MEATBALLS

Kebas

Ingredients

1-1/2 pounds ground lamb

1/2 cup large bulgur

1 bell pepper, chopped fine

1/4 cup crushed dried mint

salt and pepper to taste

cayenne pepper to taste

Directions

Put lamb, bell pepper, mint, salt, black pepper and cayenne in a large mixing bowl. Knead well, adding water. Shape the meat into balls the size of kufta (3 inches to 4 inches in diameter). Line the balls of meat in a medium-sized cooking pot in 1to 2 layers. Place a dish on top of keba, and cover with water to about 1 inch over the dish. Cook on the stovetop on medium heat for about 45 minutes to 1 hour. Serves 4.

Mary Elia, *A Hundred Years and Still Cooking*

KESHKEG
6 servings

Kebas

Ingredients

lamb and gorghod, cooked to the consistency and appearance of oatmeal

3/4 cup gorghod

4 pounds shoulder of lamb, bone in, cut into large pieces as for stew

salt and pepper to taste

Wash the gorghod in cold water and drain it. Wash the meat in cold water and combine it with the gorghod in a large saucepan. Add enough water to cover the meat. Place the saucepan on the stove, and bring the liquid to a boil. Lower the flame, and let it simmer. Remove any scum that forms on top of the mixture. Add salt and

Directions

pepper. After 3 to 4 hours of cooking, the meat will fall off the bones. Remove the bones and any fat that may have been on the meat. Stir the mixture from time to time to prevent it from sticking to the bottom of the saucepan. At this point, it is best to place an asbestos plate between the flame and the saucepan. With a large, long-handled spoon, crush the meat and gorghod mixture against the inside of the saucepan. This should be done as often as possible without tiring your arm too much. Continue cooking for several hours until the meat and the gorghod are well blended. Add water as needed when the mixture thickens.

Butter sauce
1/4 pound butter
1 teaspoon paprika
cumin

Melt the butter in a small saucepan, add the paprika and stir well. When serving the keshkeg, make a well in the center, and pour in 1 to 2 tablespoons of the hot butter. Sprinkle lightly with cumin.

The Armenian Cookbook

FOWL

CHICKEN ARARAT

Fowl

Ingredients

Two 1/2 pound fryers

1 glass sherry

1/2 pound fresh mushrooms

1 cupful chopped onions

2 cupfuls milk or cream

1/2 pound butter or 1 cupful

3 tablespoonfuls flour

2 cupfuls chicken soup stock

salt and pepper

Directions

Cut each chicken into 8 pieces. Fry in 1/2 of the butter and place in baking pan. Add sherry, salt and pepper. Sauté onions and mushrooms in the same butter, and simmer until tender. Pour over chicken, add chicken stock and simmer. Brown flour in rest of butter, adding cream or milk to make a smooth sauce. Pour this over the chicken when serving it, and sprinkle generously with chopped parsley.

George Mardikian, Dinner at Omar Khayyam's

CHICKEN WINGS

Fowl

Ingredients

1/4 pound (1 cube) butter
   or margarine, melted

1 cup soy sauce

1 cup brown sugar

3/4 cup water

3 tablespoons dry mustard

4 packages chicken wings

Directions

If wingtips are present, remove and use for another purpose or discard. For main dish, leave joints together. For hors d'oeuvres, disjoint wings (this is your choice.) Mix all ingredients well and pour over chicken wings; marinate overnight. Place in 9-inch by 13-inch pan. Bake in 375 degree oven for about 1 hour, basting a few times with marinade.

Mary Elia, A Hundred Years and Still Cooking

EASY SOU BOEREG

Fowl

Ingredients

1 pound filo dough
1-1/2 pounds jack cheese, grated
1/2 pound butter, melted
2 eggs, beaten
parsley, as desired or
1 package frozen chopped
spinach, thawed, for
something different

Topping:
2 eggs, beaten
1 cup milk
1/2 cube butter, melted

Directions

Butter bottom and sides of 9-ionch by 13-inch pan and place dough on bottom, cut to size of pan. Brush sparingly every 2 sheets of dough with melted butter until 16 sheets are used. Do not brush the 16th sheet. Also, use scraps to make full sheets. Mix grated cheese with eggs and parsley and spread on dough. This will be on the 16th sheet. Place remaining sheets (should be another 16), brush every 2 sheets sparingly with butter on top of cheese mixture. Butter the top sheet completely. Freeze, if desired.

When ready to bake, thaw for a couple of hours at room temperature, and cut into desired pieces. Combine topping ingredients and pour over top. Should absorb topping mixture for at least 1 hour before baking. Bake at 350 degrees until golden brown (approximately 25 to 30 minutes.)

Joyce Bedrosian, A Hundred Years and Still Cooking

Now, there is something the Armenians and the Turks and Kurds, and surely the Arabs and a few other people, consider basic too: the Armenians call it bulghour. This is a brown cereal. It's boiled cracked wheat dried brown in the sun. If the wheat is cracked into a fairly large size, it is used for pilaf. I like it far better than I like rice, which I like quite well. You can do anything with bulghour, mix anything with it, that is, but the usual procedure is to fry a couple of cups of it in butter, pour over a couple of cups of clear broth of any kind, or if there is no broth, boiling water and cut up two or three big brown onions into it, and eat it steaming hot with yogurt. This is the favorite dish of the peasants everywhere, who generally have at least seven or eight kids, and there is said to be a relationship between the eating of this dish and the number of kids in the family....

The Eaters, *Here Comes There Goes You Know Who*

BULGUR PILAF

Fowl

Ingredients

This is a Delicious Side Dish to any Armenian Dish, or Chicken, Beef or Lamb.

1 cube butter or margarine
2 tablespoons oil
2 cups fine egg noodles
1/2 onion grated
2 cups #4 bulgur (coarse)
5 cups chicken broth or
   1– 49-1/2 ounce can Swanson's
   chicken broth
3-4 chicken bouillon cubes
1/4 teaspoon poultry seasoning
1/4 teaspoon Lawry's garlic salt
1/4 teaspoon black pepper

Directions

In a 6 or 8 quart pan, melt butter over medium-low heat, adding oil to prevent burning. Brown noodles in butter over medium heat, stirring constantly. Add onion and stir. Add bulgur and stir. Add chicken broth, bouillion, poultry seasoning, garlic salt and pepper and stir. Bring to a boil, cover and lower heat to low. Cook 27 minutes. Taste to see if the bulgur is soft. Let stand 10 to 15 minutes before serving. Serves 8.

Karen Daoudian, *A Hundred Years and Still Cooking*

DESSERTS

Among the leaves I saw the pears, fat and yellow and red, full of it, the stuff of life, from the sun, and I wanted. It was a thing they could not speak about in the second grade because they hadn't found words for it yet. They spoke only of the easiest things, but pears were basic and not easy to speak of except as pears. If they spoke of pears at all they would speak of them only as pears, so much a dozen, not as shapes of living substance, miraculously; strange, exciting, and marvelous. They would think of them apart from the trees and apart from the earth and apart from the sun, which was stupid.

Five Ripe Pears, *Essential Saroyan*

KURABIA
Armenian Cookie

Desserts

Ingredients

1/2 cup clarified butter

1/2 cup shortening

1-3/4 cups sugar

1-1/2 tablespoons beaten egg white or
2 teaspoons lemon juice

2 cups flour

Directions

Cream shortening and butter. Add sugar and egg or lemon juice. Beat until smooth, add flour, and mix well. Roll dough between 2 sheets of waxed paper to 1/2 inch thickness. Cut dough into desired shapes. Bake at 275 degrees for about 20 minutes. Variations: Put an almond in the center of each cookie. Sprinkle with powdered sugar.

Maggie Courtis, *A Hundred Years and Still Cooking*

KURABIA OR SUGAR SHE

Desserts

Ingredients

3 cups sugar

1 pound sweet or clarified butter, softened

4 cups flour

1 egg yolk, beaten

1 blanched almond per cookie

Directions

Add sugar to the butter and knead well. Gradually add and keep kneading the flour and beaten egg yolk. Keep kneading until dough stays together. Roll in small balls and place on a cookie sheet. Press blanched almond in center of each cookie and bake at 300 degrees until light pink. Do not overbake. Remove to cool. Makes 48 cookies.

Mary Elia, *A Hundred Years and Still Cooking*

PAKLAVA

Desserts

Ingredients

Pastry:

2 pounds filo dough*

1-1/4 pounds clarified butter, melted

4 cups pecans and walnuts,
   chopped fine

2 ounces whole cloves (optional)

*Filo dough can be purchased at most Armenian delicatessens in the frozen section.

Directions

Pastry: Using a pastry brush, brush the bottom and the sides of a 16-inch by 11-inch pan with melted butter. Place 1 sheet of filo dough in the pan and brush the dough with butter. Add 7 more layers of dough, brushing with butter between each layer.

Sprinkle 2 handfuls of nuts evenly over the dough. This should be a light layer of nuts. Top the nuts with 2 layers of filo dough and sprinkle 2 more handfuls of nuts over the dough. Top with 2 sheets of filo dough and brush with butter. Repeat layers of 2 handfuls of nuts, 2 sheets of filo dough, and butter until all nuts are used up. Top the last layer of nuts with 8 layers of filo dough with melted butter between each sheet of dough, as in the bottom of the pan. Make sure the top layer of filo dough is well coated with butter.

Cut through all layers of the paklava in a diamond shape. This is easiest if you use an electric knife. Poke a whole clove in the center of each paklava diamond (optional). Bake at 350 degrees until golden brown, about 1 hour.

PAKLAVA
(Continued)

Desserts

Ingredients

Syrup:

4 cups sugar

4 cups water

25 whole cloves

3 sticks cinnamon

3 slices orange peels

3 slices lemon peels

3 slices grapefruit peels

2 teaspoons vanilla

3 tablespoons honey (optional)

Directions

Syrup: Prepare the syrup while the paklava is cooking. In a large kettle, combine the sugar, water, cloves, cinnamon sticks and all of the fruit peels. Bring to a full boil, then lower the heat to a low, bubbly boil and cook for 25 minutes. Test for doneness—it should be syrupy, not crystallized. When syrupy, remove from heat source and stir in vanilla and honey (optional). Pour 3/4 of the syrup, cooled, over hot paklava (or pour hot syrup over cool paklava.) Let it sit for 3 to 4 hours before serving. Use the remaining syrup on pancakes or French toast, storing it in a covered container in the refrigerator. Serves 15 to 20.

Mary Courtis, *A Hundred Years and Still Cooking*

ROYAL ARMENIAN PUDDING

Desserts

Ingredients

This is a rich but exceptionally delicate dessert.

1/4 pound blanched almonds
1/4 pound pine nuts
1/4 pound blanched hazel nuts
1/4 pound blanched walnuts
1/8 pound butter
1 quart milk
2 tablespoonfuls of cornstarch
1 cup full sugar

Directions

Put blanched, mixed nuts through a food chopper. Then shake them through a course sieve. Retain 1/4 of the nuts, the coarsely chopped ones, for the top of the pudding.

Bring milk to a boil, and pour in rest of nuts. Let simmer for 1/2 hour, then add sugar and butter and cook for 10 minutes. Take off the fire. Dilute cornstarch in half cup of water, and pour into mixture. Stir quickly to keep it from lumping. Return to fire and cook for 10 minutes very slowly. Pour into glasses for individual servings. Serve with the following sauce:

1/2 cupful sugar

1 tablespoonful butter

1 egg white

1 cup crushed strawberries

Beat one half of the sugar with the butter, and one half with the white of egg. When egg is stiff, beat in butter mixture, and fold in the crushed strawberries. Keep in the refrigerator. When serving Royal Pudding, put a dab of the sauce on top of each glass, and sprinkle the top with remaining chopped nuts.

George Mardikian, *Dinner at Omar Khayyam's*

GEORGE MARDIKIAN'S ALL-PURPOSE CAKE

Desserts

Ingredients

2 cupfuls brown sugar

2 cupfuls all-purpose flour (sifted)

1/2 cupful butter

Directions

Blend above ingredients together as for pie by pinching the mixture with the fingers. Set aside half of this mixture for the bottom of the cake. To the other half add:

1 beaten egg
1 teaspoonful nutmeg
1 cupful sour cream (1 teaspoonful soda added)

Mix sour cream, and baking soda; add beaten egg and nutmeg. Grease well a square pan (9 inches by 9 inches), or use rectangular pan. Put in the crumbly mixture that has been reserved, and spread evenly over the bottom of the pan. Then spread other mixture over this and sprinkle the top with chopped nuts and cinnamon.

George Mardikian, *Dinner at Omar Khayyam's*

Adventures in Good Eating

AJEM PILAFF — A delectable merger of lamb and rice, cooked in a mold, served with a sauce intriguing as an Inner Sanctum mystery.

ARNAVOUD GUVEJ — Oriental version baked lamb tender as young love, cooked in the patient Eastern fashion to merge with the gentle zest of succulent vegetables.

CHICKEN MUSHROOM YAHNI — a thousand years ago beside the Bosphorous a caravan might have paused to eat such a dish — baked chicken smothered with mushrooms, slivers of green peppers and onions A La Aram.

CHICKEN DOLMA — The mysterious East is never more mysterious than in preparing this combination of rice pilaff, pine nuts and tender chicken. But there's no mystery about the result — it's superb!

DEONER KEBAB — Layers of tender grilled lamb broiled over charcoal secretly spiced and sliced into small pieces.

HARPOOT KEOFTE — First we prepare the golden brown cracked wheat with its delicate, nutty, indescribable flavor, then we form it into balls, stuffed with meat seasoned with delicate spices. Sounds like the Arabian Nights, you say? Just try it!

ISMIR KEOFTE — We could call this dish "baked lamb croquettes with tomato sauce," just as you could call a Beethoven symphony "a piece of music" and let it go at that. But in cooking, as in composing, it is genius that counts. Try the Ismir Keofte and savor artistry for yourself.

KEHAD KEBAB — The perfect blending, delicious nuance of flavor that mark Armenian cookery, here achieved with tender lamb, fresh mushrooms, sweet green peas, baked with a wonderful wine sauce in special paper, just as it has been baked for thousands of years in the Orient in leafy wrappings.

KOUZOU DOLMA — This is it! Roast lamb stuffed with specially prepared rice, pine nuts and currants. A dish for epicures, whether Olmpyian or mere mortals.

KOUZOU ISTIFATO — Baby Pearl onions with roast lamb divinely seasoned in sauce Byzantine. A miracle in achievement!

LULE KEBAB — Chopped lamb, divinely seasoned, broiled on charcoal.

MIXED DOLMA — Fresh ruby red tomatoes, the tangy flavor of green peppers as well as the exquisite golden zucchini squash all stuffed with minced lamb and rice; the seasoning that makes the difference is a treasured secret handed down through generations.

MUSHROOM KEBAB — One of the favorite vegetables of the Middle East used with imagination. Here, it is diced with filets of lamb and other vegetable in a light wine sauce to achieve its inimitable flavor.

*PATLIJAN AZIZIE — This is a four-star dish, quite impossible to describe. Let your taste buds tell you the delightful effect we obtain by taking slices of egg-plant, dipping them in egg, frying them in olive oil and topping them with tender morsels of lamb.

*PATLIJAN CHEOMLEK — In a delicate haze of simmering juices, lamb, tomato and egg-plant are cooked in an earthenware dish such as the Middle East has used for centuries.

*PATLIJAN CHEOP KEBAB — Another exciting venture with lamb and eggplant. Little wooden skewers adorned with a piece of cubed eggplant then a piece of cubed lamb all baked in the oven with onions, green pepper and tomatoes. Described as sensational by those that know!

*PATLIJAN HUNKIAR — We take the finest lamb, marinate it in an exciting sauce of wine, spices and herbs, cook it with jealous care and serve it on egg-plant mashed to exactly the right consistency. Delicious!

*PATLIJAN SILKME — Another conjuring trick done with lamb and egg-plant. Flavorsome, memorable.

***Only one of our patlijan variety is served daily.
Please check with your waiter for the patlijan of the day.**

*PATLIJAN KARNE YAREK — Exquisite little purple egg-plants, artfully stuffed with lamb and pine nuts, cooked to a beautiful tenderness.

*PATLIJAN MOUSAKA — Another verson of baked egg-plant — didn't we tell you the Golden Horn uses this elegant vegetable with imagination? Meat, pine nuts and rare seasoning ingredients make the stuffing, the whole lovingly basted with a special sauce.

SAHAN BERZOLA — Millions of American homes serve lamb chops but this Golden Horn version of the same with its fresh vegetables, tender meat, and enchanting sauce will completely surprise you. It's superbly different!

SHISH KEBAB — Surely this needs no description for it has made us famous. Yet before that sharp, shining blade arrives, holding your lamb, there has been long, careful preparation. The tenderest filets are carefully cut from a leg of prime young lamb, trimmed completely free from fat and gristle, marinated in wine and seasonings, made into generous, chunky squares alternated with mushrooms, onions, tomatoes, broiled over charcoal flames to precisely the right degree — and brought to you, piping hot, with that unique and magnificent flavor.

YAPRAK SARMA — Speaking of art, consider this dish . . . pale velvety green baby vine leaves, stuffed mysteriously with chopped lamb and rice, and such a seasoning! Along with this dish one should try our famous *Madzoun* (Yogurt). The blend is sensational.

HORS D'OEUVRES — Inadequate title for these delightful Golden Horn surprises. For instance, tender BABY VINE LEAVES as well as subtly prepared **CABBAGE LEAVES.** Both, stuffed with rice, chopped onion, pine-nuts and currants) — the famous stuffed mussels known as **"MIDIA DOLMA"** — and then there is the very refined **"IMAM BYELDI"** (Eggplant and sauté of onion) — All of these coolly bathed in the finest of olive oil, far removed from the banal, designed to stimulate your appetite for the feast to come.

ENGINAR — The pale green heart of the artichoke, like a flower carved in jade, fresh from a bath of oil, wine and gentle seasoning, the artichoke's own subtle flavor enhanced, not obliterated.

CHEESE BEOREK — A happy marriage between mild, Eastern type cheese and Golden Horn pastry, crisp as paper, light as air and fragile as Romance.

EKMEK BEOREK — Also called "Sultan's Delight" and if the gentleman had anything as delicious in his harem he was, indeed, a lucky fellow. Toasted honey rusk and clotted cream, made exactly as the Sultan's chef made it if he didn't want to lose his head.

PAKLAVA AND KAYMAK — This is known as "Solomon's Delight" and might well have inspired one of Solomon's songs — concocted as it is of honey and chopped nuts, with just a whiff of pastry — a poem in the way of dessert.

— Ask about our *Special Adventurers Dinner $4.00* —

All above dishes $1.35 each a la carte except chicken dishes $1.65 and
Shish Kebab $1.75 — Hors d'Oeuvres 60¢ to 75¢ — Cheese Beorek 35¢
Rice and Bulgur Pilaffs 35¢ — Salad Bowl 65¢
All pastries 35¢; Pastries with Kaymak 50¢; Fruit Compotes 50¢
(We open Sundays at 1:00 P.M. and close each night at 10 P.M.)

SPECIAL GOLDEN HORN DINNER $2.15

CHEESE BEOREK	TOMATO JUICE	HORS D'OEUVRES

or

SOUP OF THE DAY

Choice of:

TODAY'S GOLDEN HORN SPECIAL   LULE KEBAB   MIXED DOLMA
AJEM PILAFF   CHICKEN DOLMA   PATLIJAN of the Day
HARPOOT KEOFTE   TODAY'S CHEF'S SPECIAL

RICE PILAFF or TODAY'S VEGETABLE or BULGUR PILAFF
(Cracked Wheat)
SALAD

ICE CREAM — PAKLAVA — FRUIT COMPOTE
COFFEE, TEA or MILK

GOLDEN HORN DINNER DE LUXE $2.75

SPECIALTY IN SEASON   or   HORS D'OEUVRES
(Armenian Style)   (Golden Horn)

CHEESE BEOREK

SHISH KEBAB DE LUXE
(Charcoal Broiled Filets of Lamb with Mushrooms, Tomatoes and Onions)

RICE PILAFF   or   BULGUR PILAFF
(Cracked Wheat)

SALAD

EKMEK KADAYIF   or   PAKLAVA & KAYMAK
(Sultan's Delight)   (Solomon's Delight)

CAFE TURQUE   or   AMERICAN COFFEE

An excerpt from:
"Menu of Excellent Food"

Translated from the Armenian
At the GOLDEN HORN
31 West 51st Street
New York

A selection of "Adventures in Good Eating"

ARNAVOUD GUVEJ—Oriental version baked lamb tender as young love, cooked in the patient Eastern fashion to merge with the gentle zest of succulent vegetables.

HARPOOT KEOFTE—First we prepare the golden brown cracked wheat with its delicate, nutty, indescribable flavor, then we form it into balls, stuffed with meat seasoned with delicate spices. Sounds like the Arabian Nights, you say? Just try it!

KEHAD KEBAB—The perfect blending, delicious nuance of flavor that mark Armenian cookery, here achieved with tender lamb, fresh mushrooms, sweet green peas, baked with a wonderful wine sauce in special paper, just as it has been baked for thousands of years in the Orient in leafy wrappings.

MIXED DOLMA—Fresh ruby red tomatoes, the tangy flavor of green peppers as well as the exquisite golden zucchini squash all stuffed with minced lamb and rice; the seasoning that makes the difference is a treasured secret handed down through generations.

PATLIJAN CHEOMLEK—In a delicate haze of simmering juices, lamb, tomato and eggplant are cooked in an earthenware dish such as the Middle East has used for centuries.

PATLIJAN CHEOP KEBAB—Another exciting venture with lamb and eggplant. Little wooden skewers adorned with a piece of cubed eggplant then a piece of cubed lamb all baked in the oven with onions, green pepper and tomatoes. Described as sensational by those that know!

SHISH KEBAB—Surely this needs no description for it has made us famous. Yet before that sharp, shining blade arrives, holding your lamb, there has been long, careful preparation. The tenderest filets are carefully cut from a leg of prime young lamb, trimmed completely free from fat and gristle, marinated in wine and seasonings, made into generous, chunky squares alternated with mushrooms, onions, tomatoes, broiled over charcoal flames to precisely the right degree—and brought to you, piping hot, with that unique and magnificent flavor.

CHEESE BEOREK—A happy marriage between mild Eastern type cheese and Golden Horn pastry, crisp as paper, light as air and fragile as Romance.

PAKLAVA AND KAYMAK—This is known as "Solomon's Delight" and might well have inspired one of Solomon's songs—concocted as it is of honey and chopped nuts, with just a whiff of pastry—a poem in the way of dessert.

— Ask about our Special Adventurers Dinner $4.00 —
All above dishes $1.35 each a la carte except chicken dishes $1.65 and Shish Kebab $1.75 — Hors d'Oeuvres 60¢ to 75¢ — Cheese Beorek 35¢

Contributors

Memories of William Saroyan

Berge Bubulian, author of *The Fresno Armenians*

From my very early childhood Saroyan was an important part of my life. Growing up as the child of Armenian immigrants — I am an immigrant myself since I was born enroute in Mexico — I encountered a great deal of hostility from my peers based on nothing more than the differences they observed based on my ethnic background.

I had no role models in my immediate surroundings. My parents hardly qualified as such since they did not represent what I wanted to be in order to be accepted as a part of the society in which I was growing up. The one role model I had was William Saroyan since he wrote about us in a sympathetic manner. In his stories, we were real people with a culture. We laughed, we cried, we worked, we did everything everyone else did, and we did it in my own immediate surroundings since his early stories were set in the Fresno area where I lived. I knew the location of the ditch in the Malaga area he wrote about. I knew the stretch of Highway 99 from Fresno to Fowler, the setting of one of his stories. I was familiar with his cousins' farm in Sanger....

My earliest contact with Willliam Saroyan was in reading his stories published in the English-language column of the Hairenik, an Armenian-language daily newspaper my father read. At that time, Saroyan wrote under the pen-name of Sirak Gorian. Later, the Hairenik Association published the English-language Hairenik Weekly, now the Armenian Weekly in which many of Saroyan's short stories were published.

A few years after he achieved national fame by winning an award for his short stories, he spoke at a gathering in the old Civic Auditorium in Fresno at L and Kern streets. It was a great pleasure for me to see the man who had given me so much pride. Even though I was very young, I still remember how suave he looked wearing a felt hat with the brim turned down at the front, the same one he wore in a photograph I had.

Many years later I saw him again at a gathering to raise money to reimburse Varaz Samuelian for his David of Sassoun sculpture. Saroyan was the main speaker. In his speech he made the sage comment, "Art is worthless; art is priceless." I was certain he had used the remark in one of his writings, but I have never been able to find it.

Several years after that, my wife and I, along with friends, were at the Fresno Fair late in the day as the horse races had ended. Saroyan and Varaz Samuelian were walking out of the grandstand area and because our friends knew Varaz, we stopped to talk and were introduced. Saroyan was pleased when I told him I had read everything he had ever written including his Sirak Gorian stories. He said he didn't realize anyone remembered that any more. My occupation as a grape grower was not mentioned, but my friend's involvement in the raisin packing business came up. That year, the grapes had not matured well due to a mild summer. We talked about the lack of maturity, and Saroyan asked my friend if it was true that the sugar goes back from the grapes if they were left on the vine too long. My friend agreed and Saroyan paused for a few seconds and said, "Well, that's the way it is with people, too."

Sometime later, a gathering was held in the home of George and Marian Bagdasarian of what was called the "L Street Gang." At one time, the area around L Street near Ventura Avenue was known as "Armenian Town." A group of people who had grown up in that area invited all the others they could find for the reunion. Of course, Saroyan was invited, first because he was one of the "L Street Gang," and also because he and George Bagdasarian were cousins.

Upon being introduced to him, my wife, who had lived in that area said, "I'd like to kiss you for my three daughters who love you." While accepting the kiss on his cheek, he asked, "Why don't you kiss me for yourself?"

Like most local folks who recognized him, I saw him riding his bicycle now and then. I also saw him once when he was in a phone booth at the rear of the Fresno County Library. As I walked past the booth, I realized I had just passed him seeing him only in my peripheral vision. I turned back, and as I did, he smiled and waved. I doubt he remembered meeting me. Most likely, he recognized me as a fellow Armenian. It was the last time I ever saw him, but he continues to be my friend through his stories, which I still read from time to time.

Overlooking a Celebrity

Ken Cowan

I moved to Fresno to look for a warmer climate in the 1960s and here we were in Fresno with temperatures over 100° or more. We settled down in the Tower District with beautiful custom-built homes. I got a job with Safeway stores as a butcher, and soon I got to know many people with different nationalities who lived in the area who shopped in the meat market: Spanish, Asian and many Armenians. The Armenian's choice of meat was lamb. I was familiar with most of the cuts of their choice as I had worked in a slaughterhouse before I became a meat cutter.

I remember this older gentleman came to me one day and requested meat from the beef called Keyma: [fresh ground round or top steak] ground 2 to 3 times through the grinder with no fat, very lean. He also requested me to sanitize the grinder before I processed the meat. This was a first for me. This meat was flavored with spices for taste and was consumed by Armenians. Will, as we called him, only trusted me to process and prepare his order after that day.

Time passed, and I was transferred to another store. One day there was an article in the newspaper with a picture of William Saroyan with his famous handlebar mustache. I put two and two together and realized that old William was the one that I made all the Keyma for.

I am very humbled to have had a part in William Saroyan's last days.

Remembering William Saroyan

Ed Hagopian

I shared both a professional and personal relationship with William Saroyan. He would come for Sunday brunch at noon to my house and come over whenever he wanted.

One day, in March 1960, while living in Paris, a friend, Jesse Vogel, called me to ask if I had seen an ad in the New York Herald. I told him, No, I never read the classifieds. He said, "You need to read this one: 'Armenian American writer seeks residence: trade manuscript.'" It had Saroyan's name and number at the Hotel La Paresis around the corner from where I lived. The ad ran for several weeks.

I called him up, and he said, "You speak pretty good English. Come by and we'll have a drink." (I had lived there nine years prior.) He didn't like talking on the phone, gave a gruff delivery and spoke real loud due to being deaf in one ear.

I went over to the hotel and went up to the desk. The man said, "Take the elevator to the top." It had a cage that went up very slowly. I got up to the top and knocked on the door. Saroyan yelled, "Come on in, the door's open. Call me Bill."

That made me feel at ease. He got a lot of calls but most were from people who just wanted to meet him. He covered up what he was working on, and we went down to the café to have coffee. That began our friendship.

Saroyan had been living in the hotel 2-1/2 months and talked about moving to Lisbon because it was cheaper to live there. I suggested he stay in Paris, but he didn't trust real estate people. Our apartments were under rent control for new/used apartments.

I told him I had noticed this place in the Opera District, in an area of Armenian restaurants, delicatessens with Jews, Greeks and Armenians. We jumped in a cab to go look at it, 74 Rue Taitbout, on the top floor of a very old building, built early in the 19th century. It had a wide walk-up stairway, six floors up with a courtyard in the center. We walked up 107 steps, then stopped on the third floor to take a breath. Finally, we got to the top, paused a minute, then rang the bell. A Frenchman opened the door.

Bill asked in French, "Is this apartment for sale?" After he saw it, he said "I'll take it. I can build my own herb garden." It had French doors opening to a balcony. He dragged dirt up there to plant the herbs and hung pots and pans, planted grapes, big black grapes and quadrants.

For lunch, Saroyan liked eggplant thinly sliced, dipped in eggs and fried, eggplant steaks, Hungarian pepper, bell pepper cut in rings put on top. He loved Armenian cheese and black and green olives. We had to soak the cheese because it was so salty taken out of the brine.

His favorite food at the restaurant De Montair was Khash, sheep's head, especially the eyes. The Khash is also made out of tripe (sheep's guts) with lots of garlic, stir-fried and poured over rice or bulghar. Another was Ombar — take the intestines and stuff with pilaf swimming in butter. He liked stuffed cabbage leaves and grape leaves, raw beef, finely cracked bulghar consisting of steak tartar and spices, fine onions, garlic, kufté: stuffed meat balls. Kouzou Kzartma, roasted lamb, was another favorite.

Kufté was an Armenian dish made with two varieties — cooked flat or cooked in a broth, carefully ground out and stuffed with meat then shaped like a lemon. Saroyan liked the domed look. If he went to a restaurant, he liked any Armenian dish, but sometimes, he would try the Greek foods, like Musaka, a non-skewered lamb dish — with rows and layers of ground lamb patties, veggies and potatoes all in cylindrical fashion. Saroyan liked this as a variation.

Saroyan lived around the corner from La Boulangerie bakery. We'd have coffee in a café and drink individual servings out of demitasse cups. Bill would grab a handful of cubed sugar and fill up his pockets with 1/2 dozen or so, take off, then feed the lumps to horses.

Saroyan told me he hated Fresno, the people, their faces. I told him, "How can you think that when you are Fresno? You wouldn't be William Saroyan if you hadn't lived in Fresno. Your roots are there. Your memories are there, it's *My Name is Aram*, the Armenian town, all your adventures as a kid...." I think he thought about it. After that, he bought two houses and moved back to Fresno.

A Letter to Bill

Dr. Dickran Kouymjian

May 25, 1981

Dear Bill,

If cormorants might have their "heavenly tide" as you speculated here in Paris in *Days of Life and Death and Escape to the Moon,* while describing the death of such a bird you witnessed once on the beach at Malibu, so too there is probably a special "heavenly public library" for writers, especially for book-crazy Armenian-American ones from Fresno, California. Surely such a heavenly library receives the *Herald Tribune* or you would not have considered going there for such a long time as eternity....

It occurred to me that 21 years at this address is the longest you have been at any of the places you've "done time." As you once put it, even longer than your early interrupted years in Fresno are the later ones there or in San Francisco and New York. During these past decades I guess Paris was more your home than anywhere in the world, though you will always be associated with Fresno, or rather Fresno with you....

The most important news of this letter is that yesterday, Krikor, Aram, Angele, and I were together with hundreds of your other Paris friends at the Armenian church on Rue Jean Goujon for a requiem service in your memory performed by none other than His Holiness the Catholicos of all Armenians, Vasken I, here on a pastoral visit from Holy Etchmiazdin.

Though I know you wanted no religious service in Fresno, Paris is not Fresno, and I recall how warmly you used to speak about your meeting with Vasken in Armenia. On this first Sunday after your material departure from earth, he wanted personally to eulogize you in your adopted hometown.

There was already to be a service in honor of those who died at Sardarabad in May 1918, during the heroic struggle that stopped the Turkish Army from taking the Ararat Valley and completing the genocide started in 1915, as you remembered hearing about at age 10 back in Fresno. Everyone seemed moved when the Catholicos turned from Sardarabad to Saroyan, beginning with the metaphor used in the obituary in Le Monde by your old friend, John Hess (he also is the one in the Trib, if you were wondering), comparing you to a geyser, "exploding," said His Holiness, "all the time with stories, and everywhere he went, bursting with laughter."

He also called you the prodigy of the nation, the vehicle through which three millennia of the Armenian experience was perhaps most perfectly expressed, you, the orphaned writer of an orphaned nation. The Catholicos concluded, "William Saroyan's writing, is humanism, speaks not just about or to the Armenians but to all people about all people."

Oh, I almost forgot, your mint is coming up once again all over the balcony, a bit late because it has been so cold, but robust and dark green. I still don't understand why you planted it in plain, gravelly sand, but the crazy Saroyan mint loves it. The water level in the two plastic buckets you left out last September to measure the accumulated rainfall during your annual winter migration is exactly 16.8 centimeters in the yellow one and 16 in the blue. I know you will appreciate that detail.

Your friend, Dickran

> Dr. Dickran Kouymjian, a close friend of William Saroyan in the writer's last years, was a professor of Armenian Studies at California State University, Fresno. He lives in Paris and, as did Saroyan, commuted to Fresno. This letter, written to Saroyan shortly after his death, was published in the International Herald Tribune on June 5, 1981. This excerpt is reprinted from *William Saroyan Places in Time* by the author and illustrator of *Breaking Bread with William Saroyan.*

Fahrenheit 106

Dennis Elia

This short essay recounts the story of William Saroyan's plight on a scorching summer day in 1972, when Nature and Saroyan's fame were on a collision course.

It began with Bill's daily routine of waking up early, having a light breakfast and prodigiously typing a creative piece on his trusty Royal typewriter or rapidly working to meet a story deadline for a major magazine. At precisely 9:30 a.m. each day, he would pedal a bicycle due east four miles to a favorite post office box. One would assume that Saroyan would have elected to retrieve his mail closer to home. But this wasn't Bill's method of doing things.

First, this roundabout route offered many opportunities to explore and possibly develop new story angles. Perhaps a chance meeting with a new character type would fit into an essay. Second, in order to better explore the terrain, Bill knew that a bicycle would best suit his purpose. And third, Bill needed a memorable prop (the bicycle) to complete his persona, much like the patented appearance of a professional circus clown.

There it was, a hot 106-degree August morning, with the famous Fresno area raisin crop drying and the tree fruit ripening rapidly for market. The time was 11:30 a.m., and I was en route by car to the same post office frequented by Bill.

I drove past a man stranded and disheveled on the side of the road. Beside him was a disabled bicycle. Such luck, I thought — a flat tire along with a sultry 106-degree temperature. Unknown to me, this man was within a mile of his destination. Trying with all his might to flag down someone to help him, the man appeared desperate. Car upon car whizzed by, with not so much as a single vehicle braking to assist him. All they saw was a scruffy middle-aged man trying to reach out to someone, anyone, for help.

As I, too, whizzed past this scene of despair, my intuition told me that only one man fit this mold; who else but Bill would dress in an old, ill-fitting, black sport coat and slacks, rumpled black fedora and wrinkled white shirt in this blazing heat? I hit the brakes, slammed the car into reverse, traveled backward more than 100 feet and stopped the car.

I yelled out, "Hey, Bill, need a lift?"

"Yeah," he replied, "but what about my bike? I can't just leave it here."

"Don't worry," I said. "It'll fit into the big trunk of my hand-me-down Cadillac just fine."

To his amazement, in slid the bike, and now with his prized possession safe and secure, and the two of us seated in the car, I did the unthinkable. For one short moment in time, I proceeded to steal the stage from the great Saroyan, a feat not many people dared to attempt.

The overpowering heat caused me to blurt out, "Bill, before you say a word, let's get the damn flat tire fixed." He responded with a deferential "yes," and off we went to find a bicycle shop to fix the punctured tire.

The curtain was about to rise on Act Two of this real-life Human Comedy, with a young, and distinctly shy, twentyish bicycle store owner about to get the full Saroyan treatment. Bill, now somewhat upset with my outburst, quickly retook the spotlight and proceeded to take full charge of the forthcoming situation.

As we entered the bicycle shop, Saroyan quickly sensed the man's shyness. Then, the mighty playwright unleashed a quick volley of demands. Raising his ever-commanding voice to its fullest baritone pitch, he boomed, "Young man, I need this bike fixed now! Can you do it?"

"Yes, sir!" was the reply. Then, as only he could magically craft the wording, Saroyan changed tempo and said, "Tell me, young man, did you learn this business from your father?"

"Yes," the young man replied.

Saroyan then asked quizzically, "Do you own this business?"

"Yes, I do, sir."

> Dennis Elia has published a number of short anecdotes about William Saroyan. Each true-to-life tale gives the reader a special insight into the character and presence of the great writer and playwright. The author's and Saroyan's association may be traced to a lasting family friendship that transcended the generation gap.

Saroyan, never at a loss for words, then said, "I assume then that your grandfather also repaired bicycles."

As his shyness receded, the now empowered owner responded, "Yes, even Grandpa was a bike repairman."

As the flat tire was patched and the wheel was repositioned in place, Bill dug deeply into his repertoire of words and wisdom. "You know, young man, I think it's just wonderful that a person such as yourself learns a family trade from his father and continues a family tradition. This is what makes this country so great."

In the end, Saroyan was made whole. A young man gained an appreciation and respect for his heritage, and I bore witness again to the Saroyan magic touch.

Where you are dropped as the saying goes is who you are, at least in a certain limited sense. If you are dropped in Bitlis but are soon taken to New York, Bitlis is less who you are than New York is. But the place you knew first is at least a large part of who you are. Places make people....

After the World, after being Anywhere at all, my place was Fresno, and as far as I am concerned it was the very best possible place for me to be — and for this reason: that's where I was dropped. The minute we met, that was it. We belonged to each other. Forever. It was a fact. I was born there. I wasn't born in Bitlis, Marseilles, London, and New York, or anywhere else. I was born in Fresno. It was my place. I loved it. I hated it.

Fresno had great early appeal for me. It had a fine smell of dust, of the desert, of rocks baking in the sun, of sand with cactus growing out of it, of water flowing in rivers and ditches, of orchards and vineyards set out in great geometric patterns, of leaf and blossom and fruit....

Bitlis, Fresno, Los Angeles, 1926,
Places Where I've Done Time

GLOSSARY

baba ghanoush — eggplant salad

baki — Lenten

banir — cheese

bastegh — grape juice and cornstarch dried on a flat surface sometimes referred to as shoe leather

bulgur — cracked wheat which can be bought fine, medium or large in Armenian or Greek grocery stores

dabgadz — fried

derev — leaves, usually referring to grape leaves which are used in Armenian cooking

derev dolma — stuffed grape leaves

dolma — a stuffed food, most often a vegetable stuffed with meat and or rice

filo — prepared strudel-like dough available in Near Eastern specialty grocery shops

gorghod — a grain like barley but larger

hummus — chick-pea dip

imam bayeldi — a baked eggplant dish

keshkeg — lamb and gorgod cooked to the consistency of oatmeal

kouzou kzartma — baked shoulder of lamb with sliced potatoes

kufta — chopped meat often shaped into paddies or meatballs with stuffing

lavash — flat bread

madzoon — the Armenian name for yogurt

madzoonov — with madzoon

madzoonabourov kufta — meatballs served in soup made with madzoon

manti — meat-filled pastry boats baked with broth and served with madzoon

muedjatdera — bulgur — cooked with lentils

noush — almonds

pacha — stewed lamb tongues and calves' feet

pilaf or pilaff — steamed rice or bulgur

shish — skewer

shish kebab — skewered barbecued lamb

tan — summer beverage made with madzoon and water

tomates — tomatoes

yalanchi dolma — grape leaves with a rice stuffing

Rachel Hogrogian, *The Armenian Cookbook*

ACKNOWLEDGMENTS

David Lometti: who had the vision to create *Breaking Bread with William Saroyan*.

Dennis Elia: for his close friendship with William Saroyan and for freely sharing his memories, selected recipes and contributions to this book.

Haig Mardikian: President of the Saroyan Foundation at Stanford University, and son of George Mardikian, author of *Dinner at Omar Khayymam's* and owner/chef of the restaurant of the same name in San Francisco, for giving us permission to use history, recipes and William Saroyan's words from his book.

All true gentlemen.

Ed Hagopian: for his close friendship and collaboration with William Saroyan, both in Paris and in Fresno, and for entertaining us for hours with his memories of Saroyan.

Mimi Caulter, Associate University Librarian & Chief of Staff Stanford University Libraries for giving us permission to use William Saroyan's words.

Varoujan Der Simonian, editor/publisher of *His Heart is in the Highlands* by Boghos Boghossian: for allowing the use of the photograph of William Saroyan holding a pomegranate for Pat Hunter's watercolor portrait of Saroyan.

To our friends who gave us encouragement, suggestions, recipes and photographs from Armenia especially: Laverne Gudgel, Virginia Derian, Mary Eurgubian and Frances Radoicich and all the cooks from The First Armenian Presbyterian Church, Fresno, California.

And last but not least, Rod Janzen: Interim Chairman, and the entire Board of Directors of The Saroyan Society.

We deeply appreciate all of your contributions.

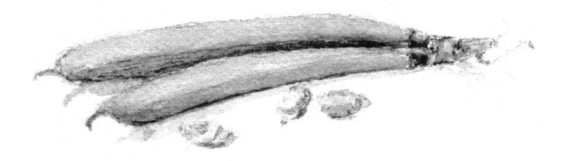

BIBLIOGRAPHY

Bezjian, Alice. *The Complete Armenian Cookbook,* Rosekeer, Press, Fair Lawn, New Jersey, 1983.

Bulbulian, Berge. *The Fresno Armenians, History of a Diaspora Community, California,* The Press at California State University, Fresno, California, 2000.

Berge Bulbulian. Personal essay.

Cowan, Kenneth. Personal essay.

Boghossian, Boghos, photographer. *His Heart is in the Highlands.* Publisher Der Simonian, Varoujan, The Armenian Technology Group, Inc. and Armenian Museum of Fresno, Fresno, California, 2008.

Elia, Dennis. Interview and personal essay.

Fidelis Society First Armenian Presbyterian Church. *A Hundred Years and Still Cooking.* H. Markus Printing, Fresno, California, 1998.

Gudgel, Laverne. Photographs of Armenia.

Golden Horn Restaurant Menu, New York, circa 1950s.

Hagopian, Edward. Interview.

Hogrogian, Rachel. *The Armenian Cookbook.* Atheneum, New York, 1971.

Justice, William E. editor. *Essential Saroyan A Selection of William Saroyan's Best Writings.* Santa Clara University, Santa Clara, California, Heyday Books, Berkeley, California, 2005.

Mardikian, George. *Dinner at Omar Khayyam's.* The Viking Press, 1944.

Saroyan, William. *Births.* California, Creative Arts Book Company, 1983.

Saroyan, William. *Fresno Stories.* New York, New Directions Books, 1994.

Saroyan, William. *Here Comes There Goes You Know Who.* Great Britain, Davies, Peter Ltd., 1962.

Saroyan, William. *Inhale & Exhale: Thirty-one Selected Stories.* Avon Book Company, New York, 1943.

Saroyan. William. *My Name is Aram.* New York, Editions for the Armed Services, Inc., published by arrangement with Harcourt, Brace and Company, 1940.

Saroyan, Willian. *Places Where I've Done Time.* New York, Praeger Publishers, Inc., 1972.

Saroyan, William. *The Bicycle Rider in Beverly Hills.* New York, Charles Scribner's Sons, 1952.

Saroyan, William. *The Human Comedy.* Dell Publishing, Florida, reprinted by arrangement with Harcourt Brace, 1966.

Stevens, Janice and Hunter, Pat. *William Saroyan Places in Time.* Linden Publishing Inc., Fresno, California, 2008.

Pat Hunter

Breaking Bread with William Saroyan

Janice Stevens

Pat Hunter

Pat Hunter, one of California's most recognized artists, is best known for her watercolor depictions of historical landmarks. Since the early 1990s, Hunter has been an invited artist-in-residence at Yosemite National Park. Hunter's commissioned art can be found in numerous corporate and private collections, including more than twenty-five McDonald's restaurants throughout the United States. In 2011, Clovis Unified School District commissioned her to paint watercolor depictions of the district's many schools for inclusion in the book *50 Unified Years*.

Janice Stevens

Janice Stevens is an award-winning author whose work has been frequently featured on Valley Public Radio's *Valley Writers Read*. Stevens also teaches memoir writing to military veterans and has compiled two volumes of military service memoirs by San Joaquin Valley Veterans: *Stories of Service: Valley Veterans Remember World War II* and *Stories of Service, Volume II: Valley Veterans Remember World War II, Korea, Vietnam, and the Cold War*. In honor of her work with veterans, Stevens has received the *Certificate of Award for Women in American History* from the Daughters of the American Revolution.

Hunter and Stevens, co-owners of Gallery II in Fresno, California, have collaborated on numerous books featuring Hunter's watercolors, including *Fresno's Architectural Past, Volume I and Volume II; William Saroyan: Places in Time; Remembering the California Missions;* and *An Artist and a Writer Travel Highway 1 North, Central and South.*